MANAGEMENT
IN TIMES OF WAR

Leadership Examples from Ukraine's Government and Private Sector

Kostiantyn Koshelenko

Helion & Company

Helion & Company Limited
Unit 8 Amherst Business Centre
Budbrooke Road
Warwick
CV34 5WE
England
Tel. 01926 499619
Email: info@helion.co.uk
Website: www.helion.co.uk
X (formerly Twitter): @Helionbooks
Facebook: @HelionBooks
Visit our blog at http://blog.helion.co.uk/

This edition published by Helion & Company 2024. Originally published by
Ultimate Beneficiary Publishing, Kyiv, Ukraine 2024
Editor O.M. Kobets; proofreader B. Issel; typesetting I.V. Dunets
Cover designed by K.V. Severin
Text © Kostiantyn Koshelenko/Ultimate Beneficiary Publishing 2024. All
materials are used in the book with the knowledge and permission of
contributors.

ISBN 978-1-804516-34-8

British Library Cataloguing-in-Publication Data.
A catalogue record for this book is available from the British Library.

For details of other titles published by Helion & Company Limited, contact
the above address, or visit our website: http://www.helion.co.uk

We always welcome receiving book proposals from prospective authors.

CONTENTS

This book is dedicated to my wife, Olha, and my children, Stanislav and Victoriia – the sources of my inspiration and support.

24% OF ROYALTIES IN 2024 GOES TO THE OFFICIAL FUNDRAISING PLATFORM OF UKRAINE

UNITED24

FOREWORD
Передмова

Daniel F. Runde
Author «The American Imperative: Reclaiming Global Leadership through Soft Power» and Senior Vice President, Center for Strategic and International Studies

Kostiantyn Koshelenko's new book is a fascinating read about leadership and management in a period of extreme challenge - Russia's illegal invasion of Ukraine. Ukraine is defending itself while also making changes in its society as it takes hard but necessary steps to ensure its future in the West. This book captures the thinking and strategies of one of Ukraine's senior leaders.

Oleksandr Novikov
Head of the Ukrainian National Agency for the Prevention of Corruption

Since February 24, 2022, Ukrainians, and leaders of Ukrainian organizations and networks, have exhibited remarkable resilience, surpassing the expectations of governments worldwide.

This book delves into the organized and sometimes decentralized efforts contributing to their large-scale success against russia, the largest military and propaganda machine in the eastern hemisphere.

It highlights the secrets of effective counteraction, making it a vital resource not just for documenting experiences, but also for enhancing the resilience of other democracies facing similar challenges. The significance of this book extends beyond mere survival; it aims to scale up results, empowering Ukraine, and the principles of freedom and democracy globally, to win. Its goal is to ensure future generations can study history without the shadow of World War III looming over them, offering practical tools for such a victory. These tools, encapsulated within the pages of «Management in Times of War,» are instrumental for shaping a future where humanity can thrive.

Antonio Garcia

PhD, MBA, PMP Senior manager in the Scottish Government Civil Service, Open University Tutor, former Army Officer in South African National Defence Force.

A good and interesting read. The book's strength is the perspective it adds which is embodied and summarised in the title, «Management in times of War."

I enjoyed the book. It chimes with and reinforces much of what I teach at Open University Business School, what I experience in managing a large team (although in a country not at war), and what I was taught when earning my MBA.

In that sense, the book appeals to the practitioner and the student of management.

It adds value as leadership has a huge contextual aspect and requires in-depth discussion in times of conflict and war. This book adds to the body of knowledge and is an excellent contribution.

Shane O'Neal

IT professional, former medical professional, and amateur writer who lives in San Antonio, Texas. O'Neal is the author of "Diary of a Respiratory Therapist: 30 Days in NOLA at the beginning of the COVID-19 Pandemic", a short, biographical account of his time in New Orleans. He travelled to Ukraine for three months in 2022 to teach First Aid to Ukrainian civilians.

It has been my privilege to preview this book and help out with proofreading. There are lessons here that apply to people management during any stressful time, including war.

Corporate layoffs, natural disasters, pandemics, and political turmoil all have analogues in this book, though to an even more extreme degree than most of us in the West have had to face in recent memory.

Kostiantyn Koshelenko and a panel of contributors pass on their insights about how they have kept their teams motivated, innovating and producing quality work under the harshest conditions imaginable.

FROM THE AUTHOR

Від автора

«If you want to build a ship, don't drum up people to collect wood and don't assign them tasks and work, but rather teach them to long for the endless immensity of the sea.»

Antoine de Saint-Exupéry

As you came across this book, it stood among numerous notable management guides — some newly published, others time-honored classics. Each reflects a desire for wisdom gleaned from other people's journeys, providing a shortcut to personal experience. They result from a quest to align thoughts with those who've weathered similar storms, driven by the competition of ideas, insights, and perspectives on a subject crucial to humanity — effective management, our species' privilege and burden.

Effective management of processes, people, and organizations is the life force of any venture, from start-ups to multinational corporations, from guiding public initiatives to leading national and global reforms. Effective management can make the difference between resounding success and devastating failure. It shapes the quality of our journey, which often carries as much importance as the destination.

LinkedIn's 2023 analysis underscores the global demand for effective management as a cross-functional skill in the top spot of the 10 most in-demand skills across industries.[1]

This data highlights the universal relevance of management expertise, particularly in project management. Efficient project management is vital for timely, budget-compliant, and quality project completion, a necessity in the increasingly diverse and multifaceted team environments of today.

The research also highlights a significant shift in marketing's role, now essential across functions and vital for sales experts, HR professionals, and project managers alike. Essentially, marketing has become the art of distinction, whether through pioneering solutions, persuasive presentations, or recruiting exceptional talent.

Management is a complex field requiring a deep understanding and competency in a wide range of areas. In war, this complexity only grows.

---

1   Jen Dewar "The Most In-Demand Skills for 2023"

When discussing war, our thoughts instinctively gravitate towards combat operations, battlefield tactics, and strategic maneuvers. Yet, there is more to war than battles and chaos — war also includes the struggle to maintain order, to lead effectively, and to keep the wheels of business and society turning despite the turmoil.

War profoundly tests a nation, reshaping its political and military frameworks while indelibly impacting businesses, economies, culture, and social connections. This book explores these often-overlooked aspects of wartime, providing an insightful look into the myriad challenges presented.

War transforms the economic terrain, triggering shortages of resources, transportation challenges, and market changes. Yet, the real trial transcends mere survival; it's about progressing despite adversity and maintaining operational stability. The goal is to remain effective and competitive, even flourishing in what are considered abnormal conditions.

This text serves as a compass for those who refuse to be paralyzed by a world in chaos, those who view adversity through the lens of an entrepreneur, seeking opportunities and solutions among the problems.

In this book, I share an experience of a lifetime, one I wouldn't wish upon anyone. It recounts the insights gleaned by my team under tremendous pressure. We fortified the durability of information systems and processes while driving progress in the digitalization of Ukraine's social sphere during a full-scale invasion by russia.

War challenged our societal fortitude and catalyzed the development of inventive management strategies, thereby fostering endurance and advancement under any conditions. Serving at the national government level provided me with a unique perspective to witness the varied responses and outcomes of managers, from startup leaders to executives of major corporations and government officials.

The skills and knowledge developed during wartime are invaluable for managers globally, relevant in crises such as natural disasters, economic recessions, or pandemics. High-pressure situations foster flexibility and adaptability, which are essential qualities for leaders in crisis management.

Collaboration with international bodies during war, and the synergistic fusion of efforts toward shared goals, are equally invaluable. Managers can use the subtleties of cross-cultural interaction and negotiations as instrumental tools.

I also underscore the importance of a virtues-led ethos, ethical conduct, and corporate social responsibility, particularly in turbulent times. These tenets can anchor leaders in their daily activities and decision-making, offering a far more stable guide than formal mission statements or projected forecasts.

I would love to see your feedback about the book on social networks.

facebook.com/Kkoshelenko   linkedin.com/in/koshelenko

This book emerged not by choice but by necessity. From the beginning of the chaos of war, I felt compelled to record my thoughts and observations. It became a collection of reflections that shaped and refined my management practices, allowing me to adapt strategies and prepare for unexpected challenges. Gradually, these jotted notes transformed into the pages before you, culminating in a book forged during the heat of conflict.

Nevertheless, I felt there was something absent in this foundation — something that would encapsulate a pivotal phenomenon that altered everything during the full-scale war. Amid the hell and intensity of Russia's invasion, a powerful force revealed itself: the unity of diverse individuals both within Ukraine and around the globe. Far from being a fleeting anomaly, this extraordinary solidarity continues to thrive. It expresses itself through collaborations, joint initiatives, and support actions that transcend borders, connecting continents and cultures with a shared purpose.

As a civilian leader operating during a war, I felt compelled to capture the immense power stemming from the unity of diverse individuals united in their values and solidarity against the Russian invasion. My goal was to showcase the beauty and strength inherent in our diversity. Yet, I quickly realized that documenting this multifaceted landscape exceeded my individual capabilities. Thus, this book was born, a testament to the collective wisdom of Ukrainian managers and their global counterparts who shared their insights graciously.

This book transcends being merely a collection of advice and strategies. It serves as a conduit for global dialogue, bridging managerial communities across the world. As you peruse these pages, I hope you'll uncover not only solutions to critical issues but also experience the spirit of unity that enables us to jointly tackle the challenges of the modern world.

While not focused on traditional battlefields, this book acknowledges that each day within your organization constitutes a battle for productivity, values, and humanism. If you're seeking guidance on navigating this struggle effectively, you're invited to continue reading.

While this book doesn't cover every aspect of wartime management, it provides an essential perspective. It presents the experiences, ideas, insights, and aspirations of those who embody leadership, management, and innovation.

Featuring Ukrainian entrepreneurs, top executives, and officials, this book portrays their steadfast resolve in wartime. They continue to work, create, and manage without letting the conflict hinder their efforts. These leaders exemplify exceptional self-management, maintaining control over their emotions, time, and energy, and skillfully guiding their teams under extreme conditions.

The book also includes perspectives from global allies across various sectors and continents. Their views on management, leadership, personal resilience, productivity, and conflict resolution enrich this narrative.

In compiling these experiences, I often found myself pausing, deeply engaged by their insightful reflections, apt ideas, and articulate expressions. The task became to weave these contributions together in a way that amplifies each other, while allowing you, the reader, to formulate your own interpretations.

Working with these top managers and expert contributors from different countries was both an enormous responsibility and a profound honor. They have given this book their voice, their experience, their lessons; thus, breathing life into its pages.

This book is not just a passive read; it's an interactive journey involving experts, readers, and me — a civilian leader in a war zone. Beyond reading, you'll have the chance to engage with these insights in real-time discussions online.

Join our LinkedIn group, "Management in Times of War," to participate in more profound discussions. Here, authors, publishers, and experts are ready to explore the queries that emerge as you navigate this book.

https://www.linkedin.com/groups/9501126/

Every fourth chapter of the book is a synthesis of the experiences and thoughts generously shared by our expert contributors, to whom I am immensely grateful. Toward the end of the book, take a moment to familiarize yourself with a brief portfolio of each contributor.

Kyiv, Ukraine
October 2023

PART 1: Team and Process
Частина 1. Команда і процеси

1.1. Reaction, Adaptation, and Changing Approaches

> *"Nothing in life is more liberating than to fight for a cause larger than yourself, something that encompasses you but is not defined by your existence alone."*
>
> **John McCain**

I write these lines in the dead of night during an air raid alarm. Dozens of missiles, launched by russia, are headed towards Kyiv and other Ukrainian cities. This could have been a serene summer night, perfect for a stroll along the Dnipro River until dawn. However, for the second consecutive year, there are no such nights in Ukraine.

As the sirens sound, some Ukrainians huddle in bomb shelters, others seek safety behind the rule of two walls in bathtubs, while a few manage to sleep through the chaos. Sleep deprivation is a constant companion in this new reality, as relentless attacks and alarms rob us of our rest.

Meanwhile, thousands are stationed at the frontline, manning air defense systems across the country. Their mission is to shield citizens from aerial onslaughts and neutralize any threat emanating from Russia. Some nights are successful: we intercept every missile, but not tonight. Tonight, several residential buildings across various cities lie in ruins. The human toll is heartbreaking.

It is often said that people quickly adapt to the good things. However, the war has shown that they adjust to the bad just as swiftly. Yesterday, you might have been an office worker who demanded comfort. Today, you find yourself preparing food over a fire, learning to handle weapons, and feeling grateful for the opportunity to power your equipment with diesel generators and connect to Starlinks in the absence of electricity or communication.

Adaptation takes many forms. Each person adapts to new circumstances in their way, but from practice, we know that such adaptation usually leads to one of three simple words: 'fight', 'flight', or 'freeze'.

Those who "fight" meet challenges head-on, fiercely defending their interests. Others, the "flight" group, seek to avoid conflict, prioritizing self-preservation and damage minimization. Then there are those who 'freeze,' standing still hoping the problem will resolve itself.

Each response, unique and instinctive, showcases the spectrum of human adaptability. In the intensity of a full-scale invasion, these behaviors become more pronounced. Groups, large and small, display all these reactions, necessitating flexible leadership to navigate the ongoing crisis.

In my role as a civilian leader in a war zone, I've particularly noticed the counterproductive and contagiously negative effects of the "flight and freeze" responses in a team setting.

BEHAVIORAL REACTIONS TO STRESS

FREEZE

FIGHT

FLIGHT

"Flight" is a knee-jerk reaction that involves escape or evasion from a problem or threat. Within a team, it can manifest as a disinclination to confront difficulties, avoiding responsibility, or an inability to face conflict. The fallout is that problems are left unsolved, neglected, or passed on to others. In the harsh reality of a war zone, this reaction takes on a starkly literal form as people abandon their jobs and homes, relegating work tasks as a secondary priority.

"Freeze" is another stress response that involves an individual's inability to act or react appropriately to circumstances. Those who "freeze" often feel immobilized or indifferent to their surroundings. This reaction can surface within a team as apathy, a lack of enthusiasm, or an absence of initiative. Like the "flight" response, "freeze" can spread contagion-like through a team, leading to a drop in productivity, motivation, and zeal to achieve goals.

These reactions might seem alien to you if you're cocooned in a peaceful environment, far removed from the horrors of war. But look closely, and you'll see that stress-induced reactions and their destructive consequences lurk in the lives of your team members, too. The stressors might not be as dramatic as missiles screaming overhead, but they are equally damaging.

The dominance of these reactions within a team can trigger a crisis. As leaders, we are responsible for guiding our teams to respond constructively to stressful situations, rather than succumbing to the "flight" or "freeze" responses.

To achieve this, a manager's paramount objective should be to cultivate an environment of openness, collaboration, and trust. This involves empowering the team members to voice their thoughts and emotions without fear, assuring them that they will be heard. It also involves creating an atmosphere in which team members feel supported in their problem-solving rather than being encouraged to avoid or shirk responsibility.

As a leader, I implemented strategies to enhance our team's endurance in the face of stress. These included regular stress management training sessions, recovery time after intense work periods, motivational support from company leaders, and informal gatherings over pizza each Friday for casual discussions — the last being our team's most consistently utilized tool throughout this period.

When a team learns to effectively manage stress and respond constructively to challenges, it can channel the potentially negative energy of "flight" or "freeze" into a positive force that fosters unity, growth, and goal achievement. Our team wasn't always successful in this. However, during our victorious periods, we achieved remarkably potent breakthroughs. Furthermore, during these times, our team inspired surrounding teams to follow suit, creating a positive ripple effect and broader synergy.

**DINING TOGETHER IS NOT JUST FOOD,
BUT A RITUAL THAT STRENGTHENS TEAM SPIRIT**

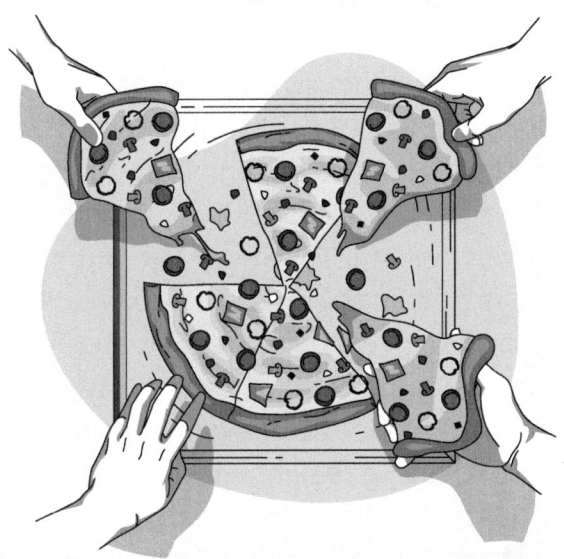

As leaders, we can transform destructive reactions into productive strategies by altering team members' perceptions of challenges as opportunities. For instance, individuals can perceive the daunting challenge of mass migration and emigration as an opportunity to stand out, take on more responsibility in the absence of competition, and gain more professional and career development opportunities. Become a hero for your country, your city, your company, and for people whose approval you cherish. This mindset can enable a significant part of the team to solve problems effectively and adapt to changes.

Leading amidst chaos is not for the faint-hearted. I won't pretend I've always been a beacon of steadfast control, never succumbing to snapping at those around me. Nurturing a culture of open dialogue and mutual support within our team is a collective effort, a shield against stress, and an uplifting force that fosters a positive environment. It empowers team members, making them feel heard, supported, and — most importantly — understood. Of course, we face occasional roadblocks, but these hiccups don't divert us from our path.

In the face of adversity, it's essential to cultivate fortitude and to replace the instinctive "flight" or "freeze" responses with proactive strategies like seeking support, problem-solving, and positive thinking. The more fervent and self-reliant your team is, the better equipped it is to weather the storm.

Transitioning to such management strategies isn't a swift, uniform process. Teams require time to adjust to this new mindset and to learn to face challenges head-on. However, with patience, support, and a resilient spirit, they can transform into robust, adaptable, and effective units. Such teams don't merely survive; they regenerate, improve, and thrive.

I often draw a parallel with high-performance sports, particularly Formula 1 racing, to highlight the significance of adaptability. Under ideal conditions, all drivers travel at similar speeds, following established tactics. Yet, when it rains, the game changes. The unexpected conditions create opportunities: some drivers falter, unable to adapt to the shifting landscape, while others seize the moment, their adaptability propelling them forward.

This principle rings true for wartime management. In a landscape riddled with unpredictable events, managers adept at quick decision-making and navigating the shifting sands of circumstance can turn these challenges into opportunities. This section of the book equips readers with insights and tools to enhance their adaptability and thrive in the face of uncertainty.

Rain during Formula 1 creates unique opportunities for adaptive drivers to overtake the competition.

Managers often fall prey to the misconception that their primary role revolves around implementing effective processes or deploying the latest technologies. However, the true essence of impactful management lies in cultivating agility and adaptability within the team. Such a team naturally develops efficient strategies and effectively utilizes technological advancements.

Let's shift our focus to other aspects of wartime management:

- Dynamic Decision-Making: In rapidly shifting environments, the ability to be flexible and responsive in decision-making is vital. Managers should be agile, poised to swiftly alter their approach as new information emerges and situations evolve. Embracing and utilizing innovative tools, methods, and strategies is essential to effectively guide teams through these changing landscapes.

- Resilience as a Cornerstone: The trait is fundamental to reliability and trust in leadership. Individuals adept at recovering quickly from setbacks are often given key roles, gaining the confidence of clients, shareholders, and partners. In times of significant crises, a deficiency in this quality might undermine years of effective performance.

- Primacy of Communication: In the context of war, effective communication is central. Managers are tasked with ensuring clear, timely, and open communication channels with their teams and stakeholders. Prioritizing transparency – directly confronting challenges, openly discussing strategic directions, and maintaining team alignment – is essential.

- Awareness in Crisis: Being at the forefront of a war zone brings a profound understanding of the challenges required to overcome them. Every victory, small or large, becomes a vital source of hope, boosting morale and cultivating unity. Open communication is fundamental, acting as an indispensable channel for the exchange of ideas and concerns, and reinforcing team solidarity.

- Value of Innovation: In the face of rapidly changing conditions in wartime, innovation is more than a buzzword; it's a necessity. While not every situation requires a novel approach, the ability to innovate ensures more effective and efficient responses. Cultivating an innovative organizational culture is imperative for thriving in adverse conditions. Managers should encourage creative thinking and a willingness to embrace new ideas and methodologies, fostering a safe space for experimentation and learning from failures.

NAVIGATING CIVILIAN LEADERSHIP IN WAR CONDITIONS

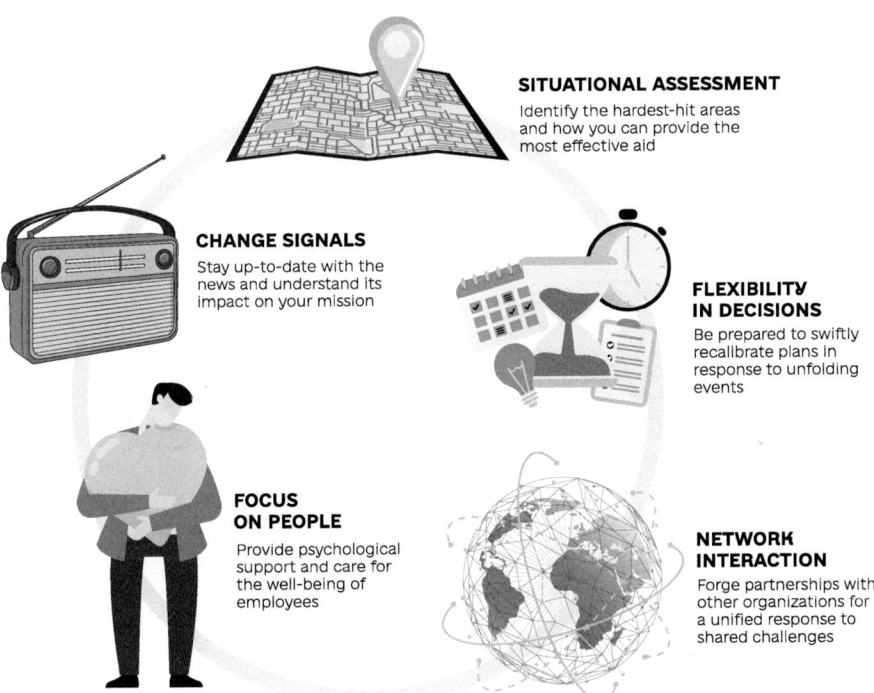

SITUATIONAL ASSESSMENT
Identify the hardest-hit areas and how you can provide the most effective aid

CHANGE SIGNALS
Stay up-to-date with the news and understand its impact on your mission

FLEXIBILITY IN DECISIONS
Be prepared to swiftly recalibrate plans in response to unfolding events

FOCUS ON PEOPLE
Provide psychological support and care for the well-being of employees

NETWORK INTERACTION
Forge partnerships with other organizations for a unified response to shared challenges

In war, creativity takes on a new, empirical form. It's akin to what Jim Collins and his team described in "Great by Choice" as the "first bullets, then cannonballs" approach.

Here, "bullets" are low-risk, cost-effective experiments with minimal impact on resources; whereas, "cannonballs" are larger, full-scale projects. They come in two types: calibrated and uncalibrated. The former is launched after gaining empirical confirmation from initial "bullet" experiments. The latter, if misfired, can result in a disastrous waste of time and resources. Therefore, it is paramount to tread cautiously, transitioning to full-blown "cannonball" projects only when the return justifies the risk.

Every organization has an innovation threshold, a baseline level of creativity necessary for survival. Striking the optimal balance between risk and innovation is critical. War has no guarantees, so empathy, vigilance, and a flexible, test-and-learn approach are vital for success.

TESTING FLYWHEEL

Agile and Scrum methodologies are well-regarded in Information Technology. These topics are worth exploring in-depth, given their prevalence in successful companies. While not all team members may be familiar with these methods and the waterfall project model[2] is more common, embracing flexibility and adaptability in our current context is essential.

WATERFALL SOFTWARE DEVELOPMENT LIFECYCLE

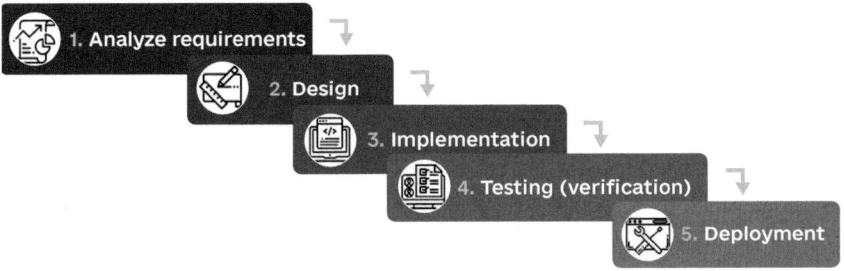

It did not take long for everyone to realize that the flexible approach, which we referred to as the "hellish military agile" of wartime, was the only one that could function under the circumstances. I will make these tactics clear in subsequent chapters.

AGILE

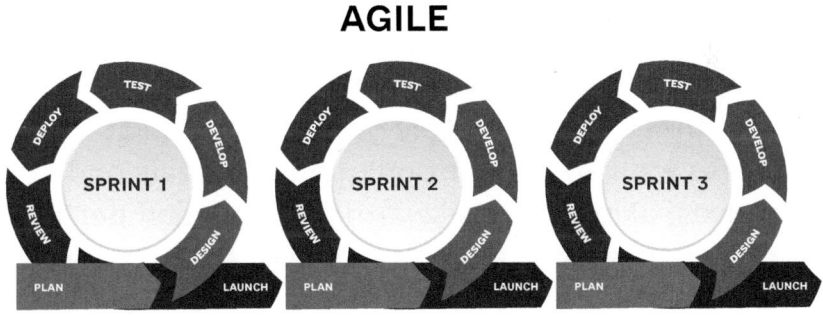

---

2   The Waterfall methodology, also known as the cascade methodology, is a traditional, widely used, and logically structured approach to project management. The waterfall model entails a step-by-step progression of a process that is divided into stages or phases. It is typically employed for projects that can be broken down into sequential and logical components.

In ordinary circumstances, progressive leaders embrace a culture of flexibility, where mistakes are tolerated as stepping stones to innovative solutions. I adhere to this philosophy. Yet, in a warzone, the room for error diminishes. It's not that mistakes are forbidden; simply, their consequences are amplified exponentially. Here, the cost of error transcends mere career progression or quarterly bonuses. It pertains to the welfare of millions and the stability of an entire nation.

Perhaps it may seem grandiose or amusing, but my father once imparted wisdom I later discovered echoed Steve Jobs: 'Work smart, not relentlessly.' And I could never quite achieve that. In the face of intense competition and time constraints during peacetime, I had always put in extra hours, while allocating time and activities for recovery. But achieving something monumental requires more than individual effort, so I rallied my core team to 'burn the midnight oil,' even though not everyone was equally enthusiastic. This ethos intensified during the invasion as we collectively pushed our limits further.

My drive was fueled not merely by the prospect of transforming the nation but also by the privilege of collaborating with those who genuinely believed in its possibility. My team was a diverse mix of unique individuals and strong collectives, akin to a bee swarm, each person performing their role with a deep understanding of their pivotal role in our shared mission. This book aims to capture the spirit of this hive, pulsating with the powerful energy of collective effort amidst the perpetual stress and uncertainty, pursuing seemingly insurmountable objectives.

I am confident that the combined insights of the book's expert contributors offer a comprehensive perspective that will inspire innovative ideas and approaches for your leadership practice.

A dark winter night. Black silhouettes of buildings loom ominously against the night sky -no lights in any windows. Treacherous ice on the road illuminated only by the headlights of passing cars.

This is the reality Ukrainians faced daily during the 'blackout', as our energy system faltered under missile strikes, necessitating rolling blackouts to prevent total grid collapse.

Inoperable elevators posed a significant issue, not just for those required to ascend multiple floors, but for those trapped inside awaiting power restoration or the scarce technicians.

Yet, a few weeks after the initial blackouts, the scene transformed. At night, windows glowed faintly with candlelight, flashlights, and battery-powered lamps. Kitchens were lit by gas camping stoves, and internet providers and mobile operators employed batteries and generators to maintain service. The streets of Kyiv hummed with the sound of small generators near shops and cafes, resembling a hive of industrious, defiant bees.

1.2. Resource Allocation and Process Organization

"We shall draw from the heart of suffering itself the means of inspiration and survival."

Winston Churchill

In March 2022 each day started around five in the morning in a chilly underground parking garage. It served as a makeshift shelter for my family and over a hundred neighbors from three high-rise buildings above. During the initial days of Russia's mass invasion in February-March 2022, 44% of the capital's residents fled Kyiv. Among them, every tenth person sought refuge abroad.

An underground parking lot that became a makeshift bomb shelter and bedroom in the first month of a full-scale invasion

After morning hygiene routines in the garage and a quiet streets assessment, I took an hour-long shift standing guard.

Each dawn, I stood sentinel at the entrance of our building, taking in the horizon towards Bucha and Brovary. After a hurried sip of coffee, a brief embrace with my family, secured in a makeshift shelter within the garage, and I was off to work. This daily ritual felt surreal, yet necessary, as I confronted more significant challenges ahead.

At work, my team and I are faced with national-scale challenges that make morning shifts seem like an irrational use of time. Yet, the next morning, I will be there again. This has been our routine until the enemy was pushed back from Bucha and other suburbs of Kyiv. This dedication reflects the resilience and commitment required in extraordinary times, illustrating the profound balance between daily responsibilities and larger strategic goals in crisis management.

Volunteering once a weekend endeavor became an integral part of life. My efforts, though small, ranged from delivering food packages to neighbors to aiding the liberated areas. I utilized our team's online humanitarian platform, eDopomoga (meaning "isHelp" or "eSupport" in English), to ensure its effectiveness and ease of use.

Our survival depended on the military's triumph. Thus, supporting their efforts became a pressing priority. While systematically supporting large initiatives like United24, I could not help but engage in targeted grassroots projects with friends – projects which allowed us to send several cars and dozens of drones to the military. I was deeply involved in the frontlines of aid.

The Department of Social Protection in the Troieshchyna (an outskirt located on the northern left bank and is part of the Desnianskyi District) in March 2023 — social workers, volunteers and entrepreneurs help those in need with lunches and food packages.

In addition to supporting United24 (thank you for your contribution as well — 24% of the royalties from this book go towards funding Ukraine's defense) and major charitable initiatives, there were still times when I found myself helping familiar soldiers, whom I couldn't ignore. In such cases, pooling efforts with a few friends enabled us to provide quick and precise assistance. The mantra 'Think globally, act locally' rang true in those arduous times.

Prioritizing is challenging even in peaceful times, especially during growth phases, when there's a temptation to maximize the supporting wave. Different projects offer varied opportunities — some promise strategic leadership, others ensure competitiveness in the current environment, and then some provide immediate profit. This list is not exhaustive.

A full-scale war is the ultimate test for any system. From the leader to the youngest employee, from corporations to startups, everyone needs to learn to quickly adapt to sudden personal and business circumstance changes. Before the storm begins, scenario planning offers several courses of action. It's like playing chess, where each player tries to develop a strategy anticipating several moves ahead. In the business world, this means considering possible paths of development, taking into account the most diverse challenges, from economic to military. Such planning helps businesses prepare for possible changes, minimizing risks and seizing emerging opportunities.

On the other hand, decentralizing responsibility allows for rapid response to challenges. In large organizational structures, it can be difficult to quickly refocus. But when authority and responsibility are delegated to lower levels, it can provide companies with the flexibility they need to quickly adapt. In the face of major challenges, where every second counts, local teams with decision-making power can be much more effective.

However, first and foremost, it's essential to classify resources before working with them, highlighting the following:
- Financial resources become even more valuable in such circumstances due to their liquidity. Every hryvnia must be invested thoughtfully. Strategic planning, careful risk analysis, and cost optimization take the forefront. And this needs to be done quickly, increasing the risk of mistakes. It's also worth looking at all available financial resources that can be mobilized — from stocks and bonds to fundraising for the survival of your organization and people.

- The human resources of the team are invaluable. Resilience, motivation, adaptability, and willingness to learn - qualities valued in standard conditions become absolutely critical in a crisis. This is the time for preserving or building and tempering corporate culture and shared values. At the same time, you must soberly understand that some people evacuate, leaving their workplaces and areas of responsibility. You need to clearly know the core of your team and how substitution is organized throughout the organization.
- Material resources definitely require rethinking their use. Efficiency and optimization become more important than ever. This may require reviewing supply chains, reorienting to new markets, or finding alternative sources.
- Intellectual and technological resources can become your competitive advantage in such conditions. Innovations, scientific and technical solutions, patents, and licenses — these assets can ensure your company's leading market position despite military actions. Conduct an audit of this list — perhaps you have developments whose value increases in the new conditions — for example, the ability to produce drones.
- Usually, in peacetime, you will be limited only by the budget and decisions of supervisory bodies, members of which will recall the smart hedgehog principle mentioned by Jim Collins in the book "From Good to Great". The principle that comes from the essay "The Hedgehog and the Fox" where Isaiah Berlin divided the world into "hedgehogs" and "foxes," based on an ancient Greek parable: the fox knows many things, the hedgehog knows one big thing.

THE INTERSECTION OF IMPORTANT KNOWLEDGE

During wartime, the demand for frugality in time, finances, and other resources intensifies. Without consultations with financial experts, you automatically lose budgets for projects without cancelling them, and you also initiate new force majeure projects. You lose people — some go to war, some can't keep up with the pace, and others simply cannot overcome PTSD or their emotions from everything happening around them.

Only clear prioritization, extreme frugality coupled with monitoring bottlenecks, intelligent resource redistribution, and fanatical fundraising can help partially overcome these difficulties. Even without war, simply living in a world where frequent changes become reality and where time and resources are inseparable from each other, every leader faces the task of effective management under limited conditions. Have you ever thought about how great strategies unfold on a chessboard? Chess is not just a game, but a mirror of military tactics, a reflection of the struggle for dominance and resources.

Imagine for a moment that each partner, employee, or material resource is a chess piece, each with its unique characteristics and potential. Just as a knight can only move in an "L" shape, your marketing specialist has a unique set of skills that makes him indispensable in certain situations. However, to achieve success, you need to determine where and when these specialists should act.

Also, remember time – an unrenewable resource. In chess, the clock ticks regardless of whether the player is ready to move. In business tasks during war, where decisions need to be made instantly, proper time allocation is fundamental.

Finally, but no less importantly, is the question of processes. In chess, the game unfolds according to certain rules and strategies. Managing a company also requires clear structure, optimization, and systematization of actions. Only in this way can you ensure that every resource, whether it be time, people, or finances, is used appropriately.

In situations characterized by instability and uncertainty, such as war, every resource of a company – from finances to human capital – requires a special approach. Portfolio theory suggests considering all company resources as a harmonious asset, and structuring their distribution to optimize the overall effect.

Each resource, whether human capital, finances, time, or technology, has its own "cost" and "risk." It is important to understand these parameters to distribute resources rationally. Try to analyze your resources. Define "risk" and "return" for each of them. For example, investing in a new project may have a high risk due to uncertainty but potentially high returns. This analysis will help you understand where to better invest limited resources.

Imagine your company as a large country with different regions and cities. War can break out on part of the borders of this country at any time. Which territories, areas, or key points do you need to protect first? The placement of your defensive resources should reflect these priorities. It applies to analyzing your business: where are your critical assets, key customers, and production capacities? Your resource allocation strategy should protect these elements first, as well as expand opportunities to ensure stable income and growth during conflict. Real leadership begins when resources end.

In wartime conditions, where routine processes can be destroyed, it is important to identify and understand your limitations and your efficiency depends on how you adapt to them. Eliyahu M. Goldratt's Theory of Constraints says that every system has its bottleneck or constraint that determines its performance. There are specific points that limit overall productivity and efficiency. In wartime, it becomes particularly relevant, as one weak spot can lead to catastrophic consequences. This could be a slow production stage, limited IT resources, or a lack of key skills among employees. It could also be key suppliers, regions, or technologies.

To cope with this, it is important not only to identify these bottlenecks but also to develop strategies to overcome them. This could be additional funding, reallocation of resources, adopting new technologies, or even collaboration with external partners. In wartime conditions, where resources are limited, identifying and optimizing these constraints can be the difference between success and failure.

Identify the most vulnerable stages of production. For example, if your company depends on the supply of raw materials from a particular region, consider finding alternative sources of supply or developing an action plan in case of disruptions.

Investing resources in one direction automatically means rejecting other opportunities. In wartime, this choice becomes particularly relevant. For example, by investing finances in the defense of production capacities in one region, you may give up the opportunity to expand into new markets. Always consider the long-term perspective when distributing resources.

Quick adaptation and flexibility are key to success in changing conditions, such as war. Apply an agile approach – create flexible strategies to respond to unforeseen circumstances. This can include quickly changing suppliers, refocusing advertising campaigns, or changing production processes on the fly. Using principles of agile methodology, such as Scrum or Kanban, can help teams respond more quickly to changes.

Lviv, September 2023. Despite being in less-than-ideal physical shape, I have recommenced my morning runs for several months now, striving to regain my former vigor. As I pound the cobblestones underfoot, a mixture of awe and apprehension consumes me. I marvel at the architectural grandeur of the city, while the daunting distance ahead stirs a sense of trepidation in my heart.

The route used by the Lviv Unbreakable Half Marathon, by my reckoning, is the most challenging, with its uneven surface and fluctuating elevation. Just like navigating business uncertainties, completing this marathon requires constant adaptation and judicious allocation of one's resources. The hills echo the trials in business - it takes sheer willpower and optimal utilization of resources to overcome them. Yet, with strategic planning and prudent energy expenditure, relief follows the uphill struggle, offering an opportunity to regain strength and accelerate.

Achieving the goal at the starting line demands more than just running; it requires tactical maneuvering and a robust strategy, even for an amateur.

1.3. Working with a Team under Constant Stress

"The brave may not live forever,
but the cautious do not live at all."
Richard Branson

"How are you? Where are you?"

These words kicked off our conversations in March when our team was dispersed nationwide. The heart of our team remained firmly in Kyiv. Nobody fled the country. However, some members were operating from the Western and Central regions and even from Bucha, ground zero for the massacre of civilians and prisoners of war during the initial terrorist invasion.

In hindsight, the COVID-19 pandemic served as a precursor to the war, conditioning people and teams to work effectively in remote settings, a skill previously unfamiliar to many.

I observed the gamut of emotions in my team members during video calls and in-person interactions — from despair and fear to composed confidence and steadfast belief in victory. Despite the imminent threat, they were united by a singular objective — to provide stability and support to the populace ravaged by war.

Leading in wartime transcends operational control; it entails building resilient bonds among employees facing the darkest hours together. Initially, I refrained from addressing personal issues within the team, assuming that now was not the moment for mollycoddling adults who should manage themselves, especially when conditions on the frontline were considerably graver and riskier.

ready for risks, and love it when each day brings something new. Such people are not afraid of challenges and are ready to overcome difficulties, seeing them as opportunities for personal and professional growth. They understand that these bright projects often lead to rapid career growth and a reputation as a leader.

By identifying both groups, a manager can intelligently distribute tasks, ensuring comfortable conditions for each team member. It's important to remember that both categories of employees play a key role in achieving corporate goals, and they should be valued and supported. Ultimately, internal harmony within the team, complementing each other, allows the company to overcome any challenges.

Be a teacher to those who wish to develop. This can be challenging, especially when you have numerous other tasks on your table. But remember, you hold the organization's greatest asset in your hands. Their development is an investment that will pay off in the long term. Even when it seems like you don't have the time, invest efforts in their training and development.

Fifteen years ago, long before the widespread use of messengers and social networks, I worked as a regional manager. My team consisted of more than 200 people working at sales points in various cities and towns of the Zaporizhzhia region. These included several dozen towns and settlements, which were not yet known to the whole world at that time: Orikhiv, Melitopol, and Berdiansk. I had many business trips around the region, working to optimize our interaction and communication.

Among various methods, I used regular emails addressed to the entire team, which I personally formulated. In these emails, I talked about the company's goals, reminded about new products and advised on how to present them better, while trying to unite and develop the team. Sometimes I was asked – why do you write them, since not everyone reads them attentively, and even fewer people draw conclusions and apply them to their work, no more than a third of the team. Of course, this was disappointing, but over time I realized that it was normal and even necessary, as I was working for the better core of my team, which, according to Pareto's rule, ensured the breakthrough results of my department (we were twice the best in the country in a year and several times in the top three).

Later, researching business literature, I found that many top managers of large corporations use this approach. (This topic is mentioned, for example, by Jack Welch in his best-seller "Winning" and Bill Gates in "Business @ the Speed of Thought"). In their books, these prominent managers talked about soberly understanding that a large number of employees ignore their messages.

The distribution of bonuses and dismissals of 20% of employees by Jack Welch's management was part of his management strategy at General Electric (GE) in the 1980s and 1990s. This strategy was known as "Rank and Yank," or "selective dismissal."

According to this strategy, employees were evaluated based on their results and productivity. The top 20% received bonuses, while the lowest 10%-20% faced dismissal. This strategy elicited various reactions and discussions in the business environment. Some considered it effective for stimulating results, while others criticized it for its rigidity and potential degradation of the working environment.

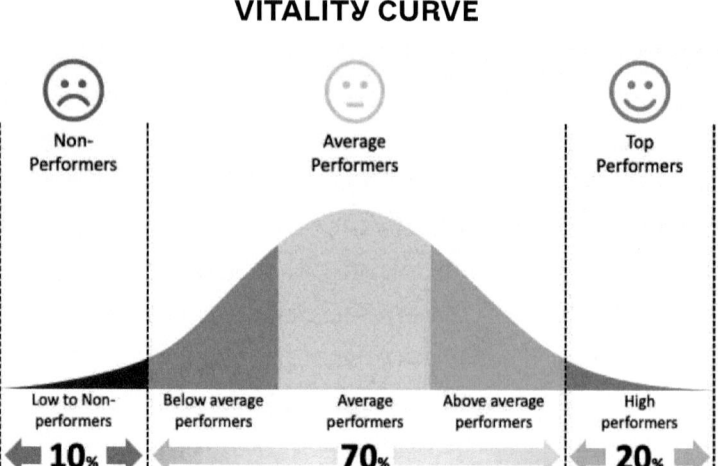

The COVID-19 pandemic had already pushed us into the realm of remote work. However, the war amplified the challenges, with heightened stress levels, sporadic electricity supply, and the looming threat of missile strikes. In the midst of this, the necessity for effective remote communication from leadership became paramount.

Here, I offer some tried-and-tested recommendations for navigating this new frontier:

1. In your communication, always strive for clarity and directness. This approach can be pivotal. In challenging times, as a positive and straightforward tone significantly uplifts team morale. Such communication not only ensures that your message is understood but also has the potential to instill a sense of hope and fortitude among your team members.

2. Organize and structure your messages thoughtfully. It's important to convey your thoughts and questions

clearly and concisely. This approach makes it easier for your team to understand and act on the information provided, ensuring efficiency in communication and response.

3. Consider leveraging short video recordings for one-way communication. Videos are an excellent medium for conveying not just information, but also the tone and emotions behind the message. It can be particularly effective in maintaining a personal connection and ensuring that your message is interpreted as intended.

4. Regularize the timing of your emails or messages to establish a routine. Consistency in communication helps set expectations and allows your team to better anticipate and prepare for your updates. This can be particularly comforting in times of uncertainty, as it provides a sense of stability and predictability.

5. Emphasize empathy in your interactions. The stress brought about by war is unparalleled, and acknowledging this reality is core. Offer words of encouragement and understanding to your team members. This not only shows that you care but also strengthens the team's cohesion and tenacity in the face of adversity.

6. For collaborative efforts, make use of shared documents. This method is highly effective for fostering collective ideation and tracking progress. It allows everyone to contribute ideas and feedback in real-time, ensuring that all voices are heard and the team moves forward together.

7. Keep your messages succinct. Short, clear directives are more easily processed and acted upon. It is especially important in a high-pressure environment,

where time and mental bandwidth are limited. Concise communication helps in reduce misunderstandings and streamlines the implementation of tasks.

Indeed, these tips are not rocket science (Have you noticed how many common phrases remind us of war?), but they are practical and effective. Even in a world of complex modern technologies, engaging a team effectively remains a challenging task that can lead to breakthrough results or failure. In times when rockets fly directly over your office, this task becomes even more critical and complex.

Task delegation is not only a key to enhancing team efficiency but also to its professional development. For experienced managers, it's necessary to understand that delegation is not just a time-saver but also a sign of trust in the team.

However, delegation should not be done blindly. Even if you always trust your instincts, it's beneficial to conduct situational analyses. It helps avoid future mistakes and ensures you are always a step ahead of challenges.

Analyze the strengths of each team member, selecting tasks based on their competencies and professional aspirations. On this foundation, you can build a delegation system that fosters both team growth and the achievement of business goals.

Moreover, if you want your employees to develop, give them tasks that require applying new skills and knowledge. This not only stimulates their professional growth but also helps the team stay flexible and adaptive to changes.

But most importantly, your responsibility lies in communication. Clearly expressed expectations, consistent feedback, and support are factors that make the delegation process effective and productive. When your team understands its goals and has the tools to achieve them, it strengthens the collective spirit and creates a sense of unity in the most challenging situations.

EFFECTIVE DELEGATION: STEPS TO SUCCESS

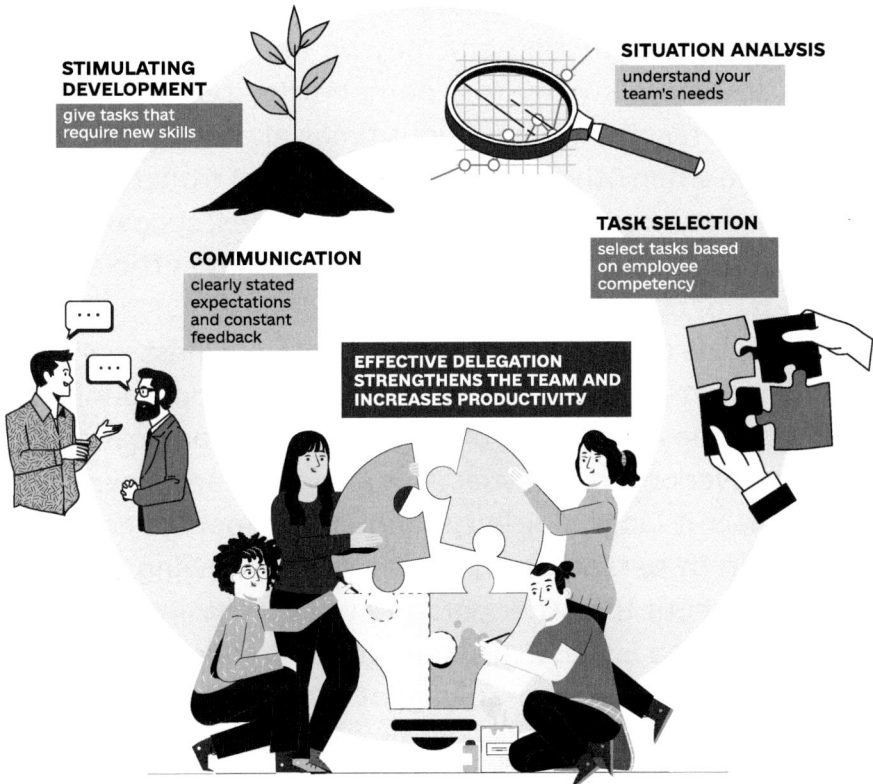

Our infographic, "Effective Delegation: Steps to Success," is designed to visually depict these concepts. It features a magnifying glass inspecting a chart to represent understanding team needs; puzzle pieces forming a hand to symbolize task selection based on competencies; a growing plant bearing various fruits to illustrate the promotion of new skills, and two people conversing with a radio link between them to denote clear communication. The central idea — that effective delegation strengthens the team and enhances productivity — is represented by a strong hand lifting a group of people or a team ascending a graph.

In the face of extraordinary circumstances, an authoritarian style of management may be unavoidable. But it's crucial to return swiftly to a democratic style, as it yields more stable results. In tumultuous times, the ability to remain productive when others falter sets you apart from the crowd and provides a competitive edge. Sometimes, success is not about the loftiest goals but about maintaining efficiency in the midst of chaos.

Even in the absence of war, the modern business world is a relentless torrent of stress and fast-paced rhythms. Amid this whirlwind, the importance of empathy in communication can easily be overlooked. A casual 'How are you?' can be perceived as hollow if it lacks sincerity. Genuine empathy requires a separation of personal and professional, showing that you truly care about the other person's well-being, independent of work-related issues. This kind of communication fosters trust and enhances the quality of business relationships. After all, business communication is still a dialogue between human beings, each with their own emotions and challenges.

In the midst of a warzone, I have found my role as a civilian leader both challenging and rewarding. Despite the uncertainty and chaos, my team and I have managed to cultivate an atmosphere of empathy and unity, one where we understand that we are all people with dreams, fears, and hopes. We've found solace in simple traditions, like "Pizza Friday", a ritual that honors the team's commitment throughout the week. These moments of 'agenda-free' communication have proven invaluable, a reminder of our shared humanity during a dire situation.

A shared aspiration to improve our English brought us closer, evolving into weekly conversation clubs. These gatherings, while contributing to our language proficiency, also fostered a stronger team dynamic. However, it's essential to strike a balance and not let informal interaction disrupt our productive work rhythm.

We live on the cusp of the Fourth Industrial Revolution, where emerging technologies like artificial intelligence, advanced robotics, and machine learning transform production processes. Our work is increasingly characterized by digitized coordination over project meetings rather than physical conveyor belt outputs. It represents a paradigm shift I've had to spearhead implementing across private and public sector roles.

If, like me, you are in a perpetual state of self-analysis and efficiency growth, here are some insights to enhance the effectiveness of your meetings:

- Adhere to the agenda and time constraints. Avoid scattering meetings throughout the day. Instead, dedicate specific time blocks for meetings and conduct them consecutively. Introduce meeting-free days to boost productivity.
- Appoint a person who doesn't enjoy unnecessary gatherings to monitor time and adherence to rules. This individual can ensure efficient communication and solution-oriented discussions.
- Keep your meetings lean. Reduce the number of participants to save time and allow for more in-depth

discussions. Not every team member needs to be present at every meeting. A team leader or a senior developer can relay critical information to the rest of the team.

- Ensure each meeting participant contributes value. Encourage everyone to come prepared with a unique idea, report, or problem description. This approach not only improves communication but also prevents isolation when tackling complex tasks.
- As a project manager, prepare discussion points in advance and clearly define the meeting's purpose and expected outcome. Post-meeting, ensure all action items are completed.
- As a team member, come prepared with clear answers to key questions. Be useful in your report, discussing accomplished tasks, pending work, problems, and proposed solutions.

In sum, a successful meeting should have a clear purpose, be conducted at a convenient time, have a defined agenda, allow for equal footing communication, be summarized in written agreements, and contribute to the team's overall goal. It's a formula worth implementing not just in a warzone, but any environment that demands leadership.

As a civilian leader on the frontline of conflict, my role is akin to guiding a ship through a storm. Every meeting I lead helps define our purpose, shape our theses, and nurture our communication. A motivated team, inspired by the tangible results they witness, prepares with vigor for future meetings, anticipating clear decisions and outcomes.

Each task assigned during our meetings must be fulfilled: every problem tackled and each change implemented. These meetings are meaningless without these results. Keep a vigilant eye on all decisions and their subsequent actions. Track who is responsible for the next steps, starting from the completion date. Broadcast key information to all participants via email or group messenger post-meeting.

When the world is on fire, a manager must be a water-bearer, not a pyromaniac. Meetings organized with precision reduce stress, fostering a sense of predictability and involvement. The leader makes this happen.

Leadership in a volatile environment presents a quandary: set lofty goals, risking missed deadlines, or opt for a more cautious approach, favoring more realistic expectations? The mission of leadership lies not in a binary choice but in striking a balance between these tactics.

When we 'shoot for the moon', we ignite a spark of inventiveness within the team, fueling the desire to achieve the impossible. This strategy can unleash a torrent of energy, realizing ideas that once seemed out of reach. But, this audaciousness has a flip side: stress, burnout, and the danger of overburdening the team. I have walked this tightrope, and the fall was not my proudest moment as a leader.

Understanding your team, discerning their limits, and recognizing when they need support instead of pressure is an essential part of leadership. By setting achievable goals, we cultivate trust and stability. When the team knows that the tasks, while challenging, are within their grasp, it elevates the group's morale. Efforts to stabilize the situation and mitigate risks may not fuel rapid growth, but they will instill balance and resilience, invaluable in times of upheaval.

The leadership that resonates with me, influenced by outstanding academics like Peter Drucker and practitioners like Jim Collins, is not about choosing the "right" path. It's about being conscious of one's decisions, adaptable, ready to learn in stride, and willing to alter course when circumstances dictate. It's about the wisdom to understand that you may not be the smartest in the room and that today's clear answer might be tomorrow's new question. This leadership style can help navigate through the fog of war, understanding that ultimate success is not a destination but an ongoing journey.

I recall the story of a prominent company leader who refrained from coming to the office when he was unable to manage stress or was not in a balanced mental state. He discovered ways to replenish his energy and then returned to the team, equipped to lead, not to inflict stress and anger. However, I cannot endorse absenteeism as a valid approach. Instead, I recommend taking a few solitary moments in the office, taking deep breaths, listening to soothing instrumental music on YouTube, and sipping green tea as ways to destress.

I am not a psychologist, so I advise seeking professional help during such times to maintain mental strength and support it in others. Simple calming exercises and coping strategies, available on Olena Zelenska's initiative "How Are You?", can also be beneficial. These exercises can offer respite to those who frequently or occasionally experience emotional emptiness, fatigue, body tension, panic, anger, and sadness.

https://www.howareu.com/

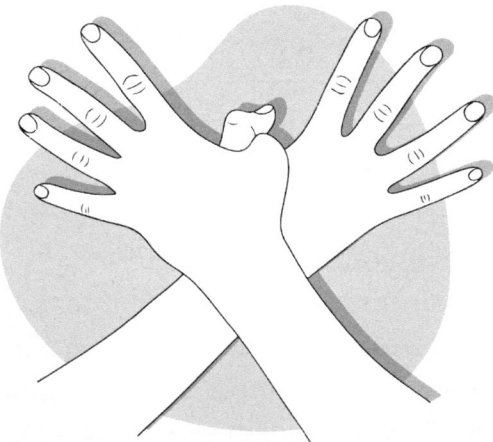

The "Butterfly" exercise is useful in moments when you feel anxious or worried and need a quick way to self-regulate.

The pounding rhythm of your heart—left, right, left—echoes through your chest. It sounds like a thunderous drum, a primal beat meant to ground you. Let this rhythm soothe you and guide your breathing back to a steady cadence. Repeat this until your breath has found its equilibrium.

As leaders, we must adopt the discipline of elite athletes. We must commit to our health, physical fitness, and rest as fervently as we do our tasks. We must cultivate this culture within our team. The more individuals who can conquer the 'I can't' hurdle, the more those who will strive to succeed in their tasks.

Indeed, training with a coach is beneficial. As leaders, we already have too many responsibilities. Adding the task of creating our own training regimen can only lead to increased stress. Trust a professional in your chosen sport, set your goals, and concentrate on executing them. This allows for mental relaxation during physical exertion, a balance that is beneficial even if sports are a mere hobby for you. If you seek improvement, a professional coach will guide you to victory.

This attitude towards coaching should extend beyond sports and into other areas of our lives. An active life is multi-dimensional. To lead a fulfilling life, we require a multidisciplinary approach — a synchronized fusion of diverse knowledge areas for progress in disparate directions.

We must continuously work on our tasks, develop new projects, nurture relationships, maintain our physical and mental well-being, and pursue our passions. While there may be individuals who excel in every possible direction, it is impossible to allocate equal focus, attention, and time to all. Therefore, enlisting coaches and mentors in areas that are not our primary focus is beneficial.

It is paramount to find a coach with whom you are comfortable. The relationship should be built on camaraderie and the shared goal of overcoming challenges. My sporadic running routine would have been even more irregular if not for coach Kostiantyn Lebedev. Although we never met during the full-scale invasion, he provided a routine that I simply had to follow, report on, and receive feedback.

Similarly, this book is influenced by a 'coach'. Roman Kuziuk, a business novel author and publisher, agreed to guide me through the writing process. He provided advice when needed, motivation when I faltered, and a target of ten pages a week.

I also entrusted Roman as an editor and literary agent. This allowed me to focus on writing the book without the distraction of the technical and organizational aspects. I could have managed these tasks myself, but it would have required a deeper commitment and significantly more time.

Our willpower is finite. Each time we exert effort to overcome ourselves, we deplete it. Sometimes, it's better to follow the coach's instructions without question.

This approach is reciprocal. As leaders, we should engage coaches to optimize our focus and time. However, we must also devote some of our newly freed time to coaching our team. We should not only set plans and goals but also participate in the work, especially during the most challenging stages where failure is a distinct possibility. Be a hands-on coach for your team!

August 2023. Friday. My workday concludes at a sports club near the airport. This location is a frequent target for the enemy. The windows of the club bear the scars of shrapnel from nearby missile hits, replaced with makeshift plywood boards.

In the heart of a war-torn region, we convened in our club. The air was thick and hot, the air conditioning a distant memory. Yet, the spirit of camaraderie prevailed as about 20 brave supporters gathered for an amateur table tennis tournament. Our digital systems team stood shoulder-to-shoulder with our international partners, undeterred by the brutal reality outside. This tournament, the third hosted amidst the turmoil, commemorated Independence Day. The locations and organizers may have varied, but the indomitable spirit remained unbroken.

Resilience is not an endpoint but a journey. It is a dynamic tapestry woven from a myriad of actions — some led by the leader, some by the team, and some driven by external circumstances. The measure of this quality may be elusive, yet its presence is unmistakable. When a team stands united, undeterred in the face of adversity, and yet can share moments of camaraderie, the resilience is palpable.

1.4. Leadership and Team.
Thoughts of Expert Contributors

Greg Sattell

a lecturer at The Wharton School, contributor to Harvard Business Review and Fast Company, author of the books "Cascades" and "Mapping Innovation."

People tend to live up to the expectations you set for them. If you expect high performance, you're likely to get it. If you expect low performance, you tend to get that too.

One of the things that makes change so challenging is that when we hear about the successes—failures are rarely documented—the story is told in a way that makes everything seem inevitable. We have to remember that things start out much differently. There were failures along the way that needed to be learned from and overcome.

The successful path to transformation starts with culture, and how people see themselves and those around them. That doesn't just happen. Leaders must work intentionally to create shared values. The truth is that change that is imposed never sticks because it asks those who must affect change to betray themselves. You must first change minds before you can change actions.

Derek Elder

CEO of Derson Capital

Navigating workplace conflicts adeptly is paramount for leaders. Encouraging productive discord is essential in a meritocratic environment, as it paves the way for the most innovative and effective ideas to emerge. Such ideas often stem from a crucible of differing opinions and robust debates. Drawing from my experiences, addressing conflicts with immediacy and transparency ensures a harmonious and efficient work environment.

Katherine Vellinga
*CEO and co-founder
of Zirkova Vodka*

Your true superpower lies within you and your organization. It is not found outside of you; do not give your power away to external circumstances. Ensure you and your team know what your 'superpower' or intrinsic value is — your purpose, brand, and motivation - so that in times of crisis, you can easily recall those powers, and it is instinctual.

There is always a way forward: It might not always be easy to see or execute, but believe that you must find a way, and you will find it. My business is living proof.

You and your organization's unique strengths and capabilities are exactly what is needed in times of crisis. Articulate your mission clearly and publicly, leverage the urgency to bring all talents to the table, unleash your people, and get out of their way.

You are not alone. Sharing your purpose and what you are out to accomplish inspires others to want to join you and contribute. It allows them to make a difference. We all work within an economic ecosystem and can leverage and support each other's businesses, platforms, and missions to make this world a better place.

Chris C. Anderson

Vice President,
Head of Content at GreenSlate

I learned in circumstances like these [of hostilities and bombings] leadership that leadership becomes more than just measuring KPIs, driving growth, or meeting revenue goals.

Real leadership means giving a damn about those you're responsible for in the workplace. It means ending up spending way more of your time dealing with the mental and physical health of your staff than driving their performance.

Mia Kolmodin

founder and CEO of
Dandy People

One of the creators of Scrum was a fighter pilot in the US army, so he probably got some inspiration from there.

We are also incorporating the same leadership model and principals created by and used by the Swedish Army in our work with our clients to enable the leadership shift needed to embrace uncertainty and lead in an ever changing VUCA environment.

Management is change management, and change management is management, not just for those in war, even though then at a very high pace, but right now for everyone, globally.

Oksana Zholnovych

Minister of Social Policy
of Ukraine

I assumed my position during the full-scale invasion. Emotionally, I was prepared for crisis response — the initial days of shock and stupor from the war had already passed. Before

with a long-term vision. My leadership is built upon three fundamental pillars: consistent and structured self-education, meticulous planning, and effective supervision.

The team is always keen to gain insights and results from my latest intensive courses, whether at the Kyiv-Mohyla Business School, forums organized by the Ukrainian edition of Forbes, or local entrepreneurial networking events. Following each educational endeavor, I adhere to a three-step process:

1. *Reflective Pause (up to a month): In this phase, I engage in passive contemplation of the acquired knowledge, deliberately refraining from immediately revisiting the course materials or notes.*
2. *Detailed Summarization (post-event): Utilizing the gathered notes and materials, I carefully document the key takeaways intended for my team. I believe in thorough preparation for productive meetings, ensuring that every planned communication is clearly articulated, even in instances where impromptu skills could suffice.*
3. *Knowledge Transfer: This involves conducting a workshop, complemented by an in-depth discussion with the team.*

This structured approach to assimilating and applying new knowledge not only fosters effective change implementation but also ensures a three-tier validation of these changes. This method mirrors the meticulousness and wisdom of a seasoned leader, intent on nurturing a team that is not just executing tasks but thriving through continuous learning and collective advancement.

Ihor Smelianskyi
CEO of JSC Ukrposhta

The key is to be constantly with the team, both in communication and on the front line. Personal leadership is a crucial tool during wartime. The war has created opportunities for

some to excel, while others have struggled to overcome their limitations. Sometimes, people just need to change their job or project to become more effective.

Even before the war, I was working 16-18 hours a day. Understanding that there really are no weekends during war, I began to make time for sports and recovery. I also started walking to and from work, which gave me an hour to reflect on issues that needed contemplation. And most importantly, I always keep in front of me the goal for which I am working.

Oleh Lytvynov

Founder and CEO of "BILUX" LLC

In the first month of the full-scale invasion, a proactive evacuation plan helped avoid chaos and retain 80% of the team. Special thanks to colleagues who joined the Territorial Defense Forces and later the Armed Forces of Ukraine, whose volunteerism helped prevent the occupation of Kharkiv.

The planned protocol was as follows:

1. If the internet was disconnected or other clear signs of invasion became evident, we would assemble within 24 hours at the office and coordinate our actions.

2. Prior arrangements had been made with a transportation company for relocating production to Dnipro, including production teams (assembly, logistics, material storage). Also, personal vehicles were prepared and kept fueled in the evenings for the evacuation of back-office staff (accounting, marketing, and franchising) to Poltava.

3. In uncertain conditions, we had two options: to adapt to the situation or to resume production in Dnipro, ensuring our commitments to clients and franchising partners for the already launched cycle, which had received investments and payments. Alternatively, relocating to Western Ukraine, specifically Ivano-Frankivsk, and regrouping there was considered.

4. In the event of an internet shutdown or other signs of invasion, each department had an authorized leader responsible for gathering information about the situation, communicating with other departments, and disseminating instructions to employees through alternative communication methods.

5. Plans were made to ensure necessary resources such as food, water, medications, electricity, etc., so that the team could survive and work in evacuation locations.

6. In addition to evacuating employees, plans were developed to protect and evacuate company property, important documentation, and equipment. The inventory of finished products was planned to be transported to Western Ukraine, where franchisees from Ivano-Frankivsk and Khmelnytsky had provided their warehouses in advance for storage.

7. If there was a need to resume production elsewhere, a list of factories or enterprises that could provide necessary resources and support was approved.

8. Training sessions on evacuation and safety for all employees were planned to ensure they knew the procedures and could act effectively if necessary.

9. Through partnerships with dealers and franchisees, a network of contacts and connections was created for rapid dissemination of information about the team's status and needs.

10.The team also developed post-evacuation plans, including the possibility of resuming operations in other cities or countries and seeking new business development opportunities.

Ivan Tretiakov

*Race Director
of Run Ukraine*

We have few people, each of them extremely valuable. Decisions are made collectively by a group of partners. We

are learning to make decisions quickly, adapting to rapidly changing circumstances. However, we maintain the quality of our services to match must the high standard we've set. Our clients should not notice any difference in projects completed during the full-scale invasion compared to those before it.

We work on orders with Ukrainian businesses. It's important for us to support jobs at our partner companies. Money operates differently d to under these conditions; our business has suffered greatly. Our team consisted of 42 people before 2020, 36 before February 24, 2022, and only 8 by August 2022. Everyone who is working is effectively doing the job of three people.

I believe our success is due to the dedication of our people, as organizing running events is a socially important business. Our values align — our projects are aimed at bringing us closer to victory. We have given more decision-making power to our specialists. Our trust in their motivation is at its highest level.

Ihor Nikolenko

**LinkedIn Mentor
for Business**

War, like the scalpel of a skilled surgeon, has cut away all that is superfluous, revealing what is most valuable in life. It shows us that for true happiness, we need very little: a healthy and loving family, the freedom and opportunity for self-realization, and a thriving Ukraine.

Professionally, I specialize in LinkedIn, helping business owners, top executives, and their teams to use this network effectively to achieve their goals, and I have a large global audience.

I've realized that I could use my profile both as a megaphone of truth for the global community and as a sniper rifle to target decision-makers (DMs) in companies that continue to operate in Russia.

What I can share now is that we have conducted various information campaigns and raised noise on a global level in the right circles to "suppress" the activities of some companies that could directly influence the course of the war.

Tetiana Yashkina

*Philanthropist and Founder of
the Weapon Store Chain "Okhota"*

Discipline and setting a personal example for the team are paramount. Your focus, determination, and unwavering resolve, along with maintaining the team's unity, are key to keeping the organization intact.

If I demand a lot from myself in terms of discipline and self-improvement, I expect the same from my team. Not everyone can keep up with such a pace, so new people are regularly joining the team.

For a successful leader, having a clear goal is essential. Without it, you'll drift like a boat with one oar, or worse, with no oar at all.

Maryna Avdieieva

*Founder and Managing Shareholder
of "Arsenal Insurance"*

In 2022, essentially I served as a psychologist for my team, which I believe was the right decision. My conviction that the company would prevail, along with my physical presence, played a significant role.

Dmytro Feliksov

*Owner of Readeat Bookstore
and Founder of Concert.ua*

Emotional support and mutual understanding within the team, along with stimulating, clear, and motivating tasks, have been crucial. I conveyed to the team that "I have a plan" and, of course, worked on ensuring that the company's core remained intact.

As the CEO of a concert ticket company, I fulfilled my mission in terms of team building and establishing a stable business model. Why then did I turn to books as my next venture? In searching for something that would strengthen Ukraine, I felt that my activities would become more meaningful for the country where I intend to stay and work. This niche is about rebuilding Ukraine in the intellectual sense. And, to me, books seem more significant than tickets to events.

Please also note the answers of expert managers regarding their optimal "management norm":

THE THEORɣ OF MANAGEMENT STATES THAT IT IS POSSIBLE TO MANAGE 7 TO 9 UNITS SIMULTANEOUSLɣ WITHOUT LOSING EFFICIENCɣ. WHAT IS ɣOUR PERSONAL EFFECTIVE RANGE?

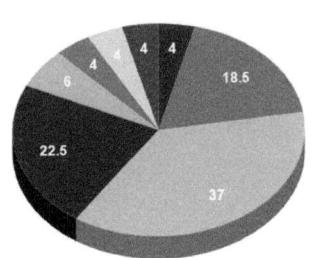

- 3 (4%)
- 5 (18,5%)
- 7 (37%)
- 10 (22.5%)
- 30 (6%)
- I don't know (4%)
- No limit, whatever is needed - Leadership is the key trait (4%)
- If a "unit" is a direct report, my rule of thumb is between 6 and 9 for seasoned leaders (4%)

An integral part of management and interaction between leaders and their teams is communication and motivation. I was interested in getting the opinion of experts on these issues during difficult times.

HOW SHOULD COMPANY COMMUNICATIONS BE ORGANIZED DURING A CRISIS?

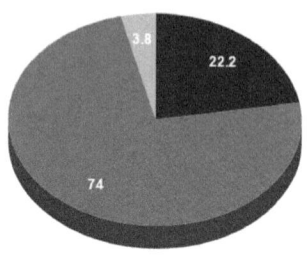

- Centralize all communications through one representative (22.2%)
- Enable open two-way communication channels (74%)
- Limit information flow to avoid panic (3.8%)

HOW TO MOTIVATE EMPLOYEES EFFECTIVELY DURING MILITARY ACTIONS?

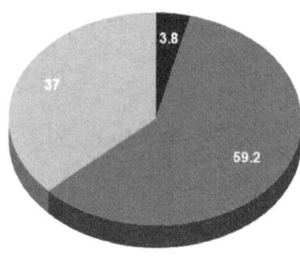

- Offer extra financial incentives (3.8%)
- Emphasize their critical role and contribution (59.2%)
- Provide growth and development opportunities despite circumstances (37%)

PART 2:
Resilience: Triumph and Tribulation

Частина 2. Стійкість, перемоги та невдачі

2.1. Hellish Agile: Project Management Under Constraints

> *Life is too short for non-WOW projects.*
>
> **Tom Peters**

One and a half months before the start of the full-scale invasion. I enter my office early, only to find it already bustling. The door wide open, the room transformed overnight into what looks like an impromptu headquarters. It's a stark contrast from the usual quiet mornings.

The team is already deep in work. People are arriving earlier each day, the evenings stretching longer as they leave. It's a testament to their dedication that even those absent physically are contributing fervently online. Remarkably, those who head home in the evening are back online just hours later, their commitment undimmed by the late hour.

The large negotiating table has become the center of our operations. Around it, my team — assembled for their quick thinking and expertise — works tirelessly. Their task is

team members and consultants converge to meticulously dissect and deliberate every phase, idea, and strategy of a project. Amidst a backdrop of computers, indispensable documents, visual presentations, and an array of technological resources, this command center is where pivotal decisions are forged, shaping the trajectory of our endeavors.

My familiarity with War Rooms began well before the onset of the invasion, having already established such a strategic space in my ministry office. Though the conflict reshaped their use, the core elements of a War Room remain unchanged:

- **Strategic Space:** Essential for a War Room is ample space for creativity and visualization. It includes whiteboards, flipcharts, and accessible screens. Tables are awash with papers and documents, and laptops seamlessly connect, ensuring a dynamic and interactive environment.
- **Unbridled Communication:** A hallmark of the War Room is the free flow of ideas. Every team member's voice is heard, with information efficiently recorded and circulated, fostering a culture of transparency and inclusivity.
- **Inclusive Collaboration:** The War Room champions egalitarianism, where diverse thoughts and perspectives are freely expressed, ensuring a rich tapestry of ideas that contribute to the project's success.
- **Focused Visualization:** In the War Room, achieving clarity is paramount, and it's accomplished through a blend of traditional and Agile visualization tools. It includes Gantt Charts for detailed timeline tracking, analytical

data for in-depth project analysis, Burndown Charts to monitor sprint progress by comparing completed work against what's pending, Cumulative Flow Diagrams for a visual representation of work status over time, and Kanban Boards to dynamically visualize tasks and workflow, helping in effective team coordination and project management.

- **Diverse Perspectives:** The War Room becomes a crucible for comprehensive project overview and decision-making by incorporating views from various departments and fields.

Project management in a warzone is a formidable challenge, a delicate balancing act between urgent, nationally significant tasks and routine yet central ones. The allocation of time, resources, and energy between these tasks can unexpectedly dictate the success of the project. The thrill of executing exhilarating projects fuels the team, fostering active engagement and tenacity in the face of adversity.

As a civilian leader, I spearheaded the development of the humanitarian platform eSupport. This project became a symbol of optimism, exemplifying our capacity for innovation, forging new paths, and relentless pursuit of noble goals. We birthed effective, groundbreaking solutions, each a potent weapon in our fight for survival.

Yet, it is vital to acknowledge the importance of the "mundane" tasks. They form the backbone of our operations, providing fundamental stability. These tasks might lack the thrill of the novel and innovation, but they are the gears that keep the mechanism of our operations functioning. As leaders, we must inspire our team to appreciate the value of these tasks, and to understand their significance amidst the chaos. Effective leadership shines brightest under conditions of stress and scarce resources.

Our innovative projects are more than just tasks to be completed; they are motivational powerhouses. They inspire our existing team and act as magnets for new talent. Every project we undertake echoes with the promise of change, of making a difference. We delve deep into their impact, studying their ripple effects. We enhance the positive, mitigate the negative, and always strive for a broader influence.

For instance, when we introduced electronic documents through Diia-sharing in our social protection offices, we aimed to simplify our citizens' lives. However, the implementation also alleviated the burden on office employees and streamlined their operations. We faced resistance initially, as old habits die hard. Nonetheless, we chose innovation over persuasion, altering the interface to promote the use of digital documents. The result was an exponential surge in usage and not a single complaint from our employees.

Sometimes, a project may not seem impactful or may not stir your soul, but even the slightest positive impact is a victory. We strive to innovate, to turbo-boost the effect of each project tenfold without a corresponding cost increase. With this approach, even the most humble project can exceed expectations and become groundbreaking.

Deadlines, often overlooked or seen as flexible in peace-time, take on a deadly seriousness in a warzone. A delay can mean the difference between life and death. In this harsh reality, every action, and decision carries immense weight.

Being a civilian leader in a warzone is a unique challenge. It requires tireless effort, unwavering focus, and an unwavering belief in the power of human resilience. It calls for leadership in its purest form.

As a civilian leader in a warzone, I embraced not the paralysis of analysis but the vitality of action. The philosophy of "Great by Choice" echoed in my approach — "first bullets then cannonballs". A decisive yet calculated strategy, sparing resources while ensuring precision before unleashing the full power.

The volatile world demanded flexibility. Once a preference, Agile management became an imperative amidst the relentless onslaught. It was contrary to the conventional waterfall approach, often favored in state projects. With its fluidity, Agile allowed us to adapt to the ebb and flow of changing circumstances.

Agile is about fostering communication and connection. Daily huddles nurtured team solidarity as we navigated through the obstacles, charting the course for the immediate future. The user was our North Star. Agile's mission, to release beneficial software swiftly, demanded our keen understanding of users' needs and priorities.

After every sprint, the team reflected — a retrospective not of regret but of continuous improvement. Agile's core principle resonated profoundly — valuing professional adaptability and collaboration over rigid plans and hierarchies.

As we navigated the storm, Agile's four key values were our compass:
1. Individuals and interactions over processes and tools.
2. Working product over comprehensive documentation.
3. Customer collaboration over contract negotiation.
4. Responding to change over following a plan.

Agree, that these principles are clearly suitable for work when there is a perfect storm around.

KANBAN BOARD BASED ON THE EXAMPLE OF DIGITAL PROJECTS OF THE MINISTRY OF SOCIAL POLICY OF UKRAINE

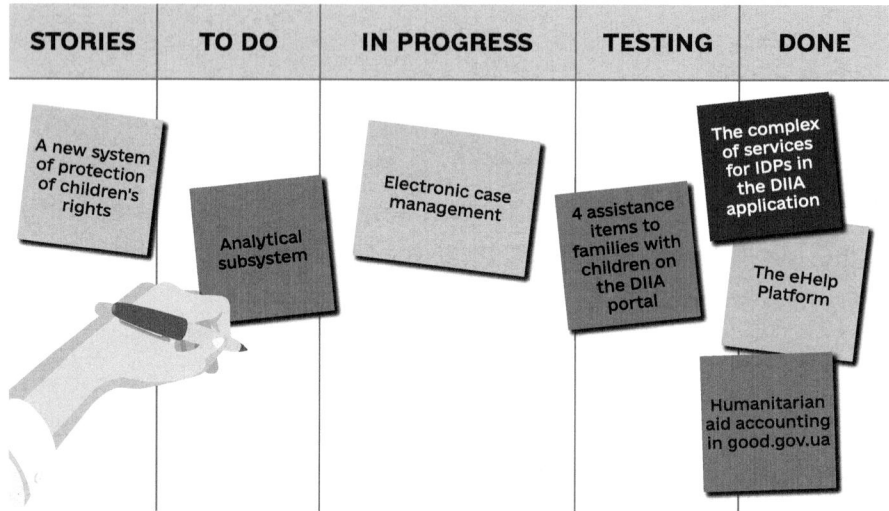

STORIES	TO DO	IN PROGRESS	TESTING	DONE

A new system of protection of children's rights

Analytical subsystem

Electronic case management

4 assistance items to families with children on the DIIA portal

The complex of services for IDPs in the DIIA application

The eHelp Platform

Humanitarian aid accounting in good.gov.ua

Our journey was marked by real projects, from creating a new system for child protection to developing an electronic case management system. We celebrated victories, like the suite of services for displaced persons in the Diia application, while learning from ongoing challenges.

Agile, though my preferred approach, is not without its pitfalls. Its adaptability could lead to uncertainty and increased risk. The constant need to pivot could disrupt planning and adherence to deadlines. Task distribution could potentially escalate costs and delays. Integration issues could stall development. And the lack of insight into individual work styles could affect teamwork.

AGILE: MAKING FLEXIBILITY AND ADAPTABILITY THE KEY VALUES OF EFFECTIVE PROJECT MANAGEMENT

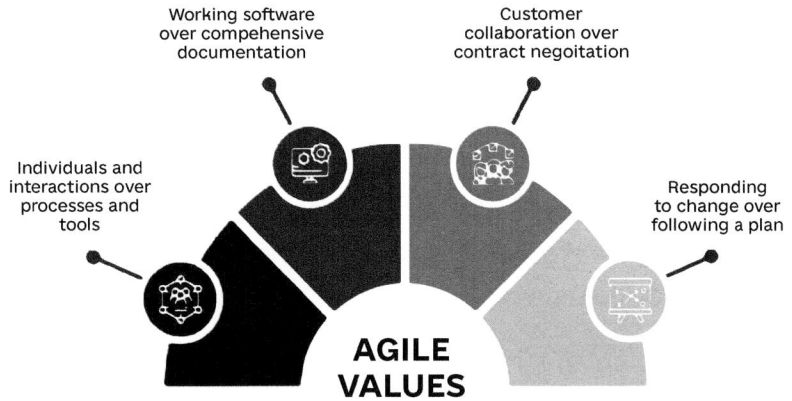

Yet, Agile's very nature is to thrive amidst the chaos, propelling us forward in in the BANI[3] world, which replaces the VUCA[4] world. It allows us to navigate flexibly towards ever-shifting goals, offering a versatile solution not only for warzones but also for various crises, changing contexts, and competitive complexities.

The 'fog of war' (German: Nebel des Krieges) refers to the inevitable uncertainty and variability of information in a military theater. This concept encapsulates the unknowns about one's capabilities, the enemy's strengths, and intentions during a battle, operation, or campaign. Military forces strive to mitigate this fog through intelligence and heightened situational awareness. The term has also been adopted in strategic computer games to represent the uncertainty mechanics. In

---

3   With the start of the 2020 pandemic, the world became BANI. This term was proposed by James Cashio of the Future Institute (USA). B — brittle, A — anxious, N — nonlinear, I — incomprehensible.

4   VUCA (world) is an acronym created in 1987 based on the leadership theories of Warren Bennis and Bert Nanus. V — volatility, U — uncertainty, C — complexity, A — ambiguity.

these games, the 'fog of war' is often depicted as a dark or semi-transparent veil obscuring terrain and enemy positions, ensuring equal footing by limiting the initial knowledge of opponents. It dissipates within a unit's viewing radius but can thicken once again upon their retreat.

In business, leaders often navigate their own 'fog of war,' striving to eliminate its boundaries for themselves, their teams, and partners. Collaborating in a unified information environment, where everyone is apprised of the situation, fosters synchronized action even when coordination time is scarce.

In the Agile framework, the core values serve more as guiding lights than rigid directives. They are meant to spark innovation and adaptability, not confine them:

- Customize Agile Principles: Tailor Agile values to resonate with the unique dynamics and needs of your team, ensuring they complement rather than conflict with your group's natural workflow.
- Foster a Culture of Growth: Encourage a mindset of continuous development, where learning is derived from both triumphs and setbacks, enriching your team's collective expertise.
- Reevaluate When Necessary: If a specific Agile principle doesn't fit well with your team's approach, openly discuss its utility and consider alternative strategies that might be more effective.
- Balance Values with Practicality: Agile values are important, but they should harmonize with, not displace, established methods that have proven effective for your team.

- **Align with Your Goals: Ensure that the implementation of Agile values is in sync with your team's overarching mission and objectives, integrating these principles in a way that enhances, not hinders, your daily operations.**

Bankova Street. Office of the President. We gathered for International Children's Day. Volodymyr Zelenskyi led the assemblage, a mix of faces from different departments and ministries. Our goal was singular: the well-being and rights of children.

I had a role to play, a part of something bigger. Under the guidance of Dariia Herasymchuk, the Presidential Commissioner for Children's Rights and Rehabilitation in Ukraine, we forged a path towards a new adoption service on the Diia portal. It was ambitious, a a shining example in trying times.

The project, however, was not without its trials. February 24th marked an abrupt halt in our progress, a forced intermission. By April, we rallied, pooling every resource at our disposal to meet a June 1st deadline. Three development teams, each a cog in a larger machine, focused on integrating existing systems for online adoption consultations.

The journey was fraught with challenges. Distance became a daily adversary as most of our team worked remotely, scattered, and evacuated. Connectivity issues were rampant, and the mental toll was heavy – stress and panic attacks in the shadow of war.

Despite these hurdles, we neared our goal. On May 31st, a resolution from the Cabinet of Ministers cleared our path both technically and legally. The stage was set for a June 1st launch. Press conferences and meetings were aligned with precision.

But life, as it often does, defied our plans. On the morning of the launch, a critical directory connection was missing. The team scrambled as Daria and I briefed the press. We treaded carefully with our words, balancing on the thin line between truth and expectation.

In the President's Office, Daria and I exchanged knowing glances. We chose silence over half-truths. The President's commitment to digitalization and children's welfare weighed heavily on us. To speak of an unfinished project was to peddle empty promises.

The discomfort of that moment lingered. But after the meeting, as I returned to my office, the service flickered to life at 15:58. A small victory, perhaps, but a victory nonetheless.

In the quiet of my office, I sent my thanks to the team through the digital ether. The outcome couldn't be changed, but the response could shape our future endeavors. Our team faced a horizon lined with challenges, and fear had no place in our ranks.

2.2. Managing Risks When It's Impossible to Manage

"The biggest risk is not taking any risk... In a world that is changing really quickly, the only strategy that is guaranteed to fail is not taking risks."

Mark Zuckerburg

The specter of war cast a shadow over the early days, turning every air raid alert into a terrifying symphony of evacuation — civilians seeking refuge in bomb shelters, underground parking lots, and metro stations. The uncertainty of the incoming missiles — whether they would rain down destruction or target specific areas — hung like a dark cloud over us. One day, midway to the office, my wife's voice echoed with fear over the phone, urging me to return home as a missile had struck cars on the Kyiv ring road.

As the months wore on, the situation evolved. Kyiv was now mostly targeted by missiles and drones, and the enemy troops had been pushed back. People's attitudes towards missile strikes morphed in response. Some sought safety as before; others continued working, undeterred by the looming threat. A few even adapted to the forced breaks in work, using them as moments for a quick smoke or a leisurely walk.

In such a volatile environment, a stark reality emerged: as the leader of a large-scale project, I was the biggest risk. The project's fate hinged on my survival, a threat amplified by the ongoing war. It was not just because a missile could obliterate my home tomorrow but also because duty could call me from office to battlefield.

A leader is but a gear in a larger mechanism. The challenge lies not just in identifying the key players but also in devising a contingency plan to minimize the project's dependency on specific individuals. I also realized the importance of grooming potential successors, regardless of the unsettling nature of the task.

I consciously chose not to seek deferment from mobilization as a key ministry employee. As a military obligant, I was committed to building a team that could thrive without me. It was a process filled with insights:

- Training a successor takes time and dedication.
- Leadership isn't for everyone. Honesty is key.
- Character and values outweigh technical skills.
- Mentoring is a two-way street, not always met with gratitude.

The quest for a successor should start immediately, nurturing several candidates to ensure the organization's endurance.

As a civilian leader in a warzone, my duty extended beyond command to inspiration; building not just a team but a durable system in the face of crisis.

Many leaders fear being outshone by their team, hindering their ability to delegate or form impactful relationships. In unpredictable times, having backups for key roles is a safety net. If one fails, the system must endure.

Strong leadership invests in mentorship, cross-training, and internal rotation. It keeps operations smooth and boosts morale, reinforcing each person's role in the organization's success.

One miscalculated decision can jeopardize even the largest of companies, as the experience of renowned CEO Jack Welch shows. Therefore, succession planning is not a guarantee for a stable future, but retaining key personnel, especially during trying times, is paramount.

In my case, the complexities of leading in a warzone were exacerbated by the looming threat of being called to the frontline. It was prudent, therefore, to rely mainly on the women in the team. This strategy, however, isn't just a wartime necessity. According to Ernst & Young[5], companies with more than 25% women in leadership positions witness at least a 6% growth in profitability, a larger market segment by 45%, and an approximately 70% higher growth rate in new markets.

Transparency in project management also enhances team awareness. However, in wartime, this transparency is limited by cybersecurity and in periods of force majeure. With the team under a heavy workload, not everyone can regularly write updates and prepare releases, leading to gaps.

Transparency in project management also enhances team awareness. However, in wartime, this transparency is limited by cybersecurity and in periods of force majeure. With the team under a heavy workload, not everyone can regularly write updates and prepare releases, leading to gaps.

Leadership isn't defined by singular successes. The leadership journey is about the consistent forward momentum, not just the peaks. It's about embracing the lessons in every

5   Women.
    Fast forward.
    The time for
    gender parity
    is now

challenge and every joy and using them to become a better leader.

CULTIVATE MEANINGFUL WORK AND RELATIONSHIPS ACCORDING TO RAY DALIO'S «BELIEVING IN RADICAL TRUTH AND RADICAL TRANSPARENCY»

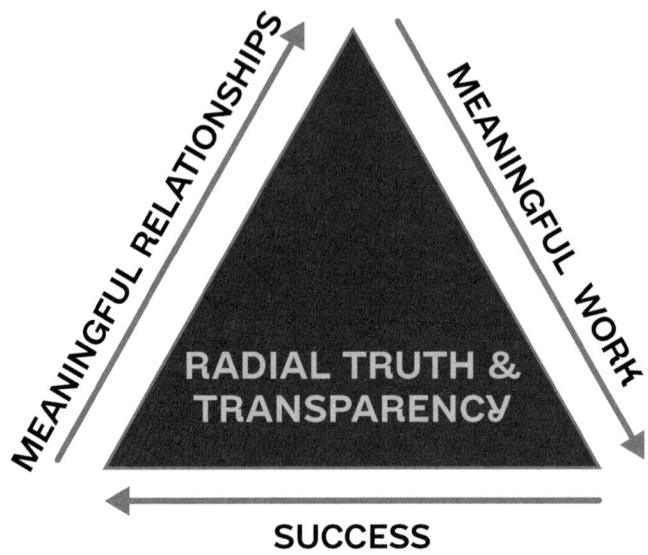

Yes, indeed, we all make mistakes. It's a universal truth that not everything always goes according to plan. However, the worst scenario unfolds when, you simply give up after facing a few setbacks. A true manager, in contrast, actively seeks out ways to rectify these errors. They understand the underlying issues and ensure these challenges don't break their spirit. Therefore, genuine success in management isn't solely about the moments of glory; it's also about the ability to discern valuable lessons in every experience, be it joyous or challenging. Every aspect, and every experience can potentially serve as a stepping stone toward your professional advancement.

Now, let's delve deeper into the main subject: what exactly is risk management, and how do its characteristics transform when we navigate through periods of tranquility or turbulence?

Irrespective of its size, every business encounters risks. These risks could be manifested as unpredictable events that could potentially derail plans and impact the company's success or revenues. So, what's our approach towards these risks? We aim to comprehend them thoroughly and strive to bring them under our control.

The risk management cycle can be likened to a dance involving four key steps. Firstly, we 'identify' the risks, picturing what could possibly go wrong. Secondly, we 'evaluate' these risks, gauging their potential impact and significance. Thirdly, we 'select a strategy', deciding how we will respond to these challenges and whether they merit our time and resources. Finally, we 'monitor' the progress, adjusting our strategies as needed.

For a company, managing risks is akin to teaching a child to cross the street safely. It's about being vigilant, assessing the surroundings, judging the speed of oncoming traffic, deciding when it's safe to proceed, and maintaining alertness at all times. Similarly with risks—if we consider them carefully and approach them wisely, our business will only move upwards. It's essential in business to not only acknowledge these risks but also to engage with them strategically. By doing so, we can turn potential threats into opportunities for growth and improvement.

RISK MANAGEMENT LIFE CYCLE

It's better to identify and address risks at an early stage. Risks can escalate, so it's crucial to be aware of them as early as possible. If they evolve into problems, having time and resources, we can rectify them. If a risk is too great, it might be wise to reconsider plans to avoid wasting resources.

SHAREHOLDERS VISION

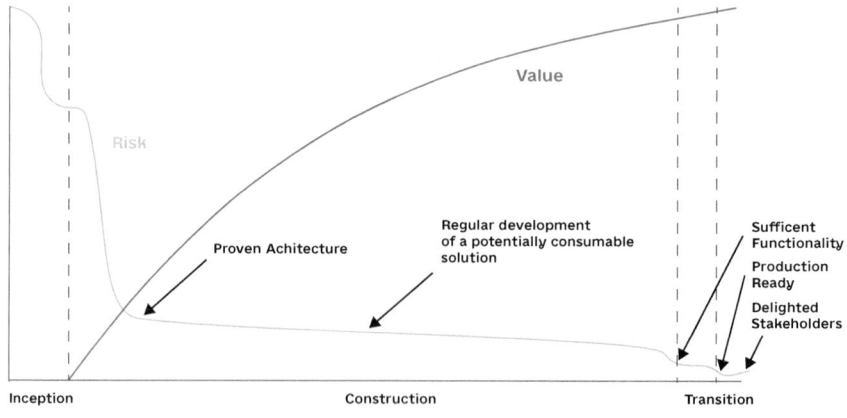

In modern programming, 'Agile' has become the main method of project management. This methodology is renowned for its flexibility, which helps teams quickly adapt to any new developments. As a result, risk management within Agile differs somewhat from traditional approaches.

This approach is particularly effective in environments characterized by rapid and unpredictable changes, which are felt most extensively, quickly, and dangerously during times of war.

Paying close attention to problems at an early stage is also key. Daily team meetings, known as daily stand-ups, facilitate the exchange of ideas and quickly identify potential issues.

One of the most exciting aspects of Agile is "live planning." You don't sit around waiting for months for problems to emerge. Each sprint offers a chance to pause, reassess current risks, and decide how to address them. Therefore, every two weeks, you have a plan of action.

This iterative process allows for continuous monitoring and adjustment, making Agile particularly suitable for dynamic and uncertain environments. It emphasizes the importance of team collaboration, rapid response to change, and maintaining a focus on delivering value despite challenges and uncertainties. By embracing this approach, businesses can navigate complex situations more effectively and ensure that they remain flexible and adaptable in the face of ongoing changes and risks.

Playing with open cards: Agile values transparency. There's no room for secrets here. Everyone in the team sees where the potential pitfalls are, thanks to tools like task boards. It's like a roadmap where everyone can point out the potholes. Priorities here are straightforward: tackle what poses the greatest risk first. After the sprint, everyone gathers to discuss what worked and where the 'underwater rocks' are. This is how we learn from our mistakes.

RISK ANALYSIS WITH FLEXIBLE PLANNING

BACKLOG	TO DO	IN PROGRESS	TESTING	DONE

Launch an online service in the metaverse.

Risk: Few citizens possess glasses that enable full use of the technology.

Automate the appointment of social assistance.

Risk: a failure in the calculation can deprive someone of payments.

Use manual application forms for types of social assistance that are not automated.

Risk: There is subjectivity in employee determinations and lengthy manual review periods.

Implement electronic case management for social services.

Risk: Employees accustomed to the manual paper process might ignore the new system or enter incorrect data.

Introduce new functionality of the social sphere's digital system.

Risk: Not all errors are detected at the testing stage, and they may occur unexpectedly in the system operation.

When we talk about 'stories to do', 'doing', and 'done' in the context of risk management in Agile:

Backlog: At this stage, the team identifies potential risks that may arise during task execution. Identifying risks early on allows for planning preventative measures or strategies for their minimization.

To Do: The project incorporates components that help minimize risks, monitor them, and respond if they materialize.

Doing: Here, the team actively works on the task and monitors the risks identified at the beginning. If a new risk emerges or an existing one becomes a threat, the team can quickly respond and adjust their actions.

Done: When a task reaches completion, the team analyses their risk management strategies during execution.

This process aids in extracting lessons and preparing for subsequent tasks. It is also essential to confirm whether risks were effectively minimized. Moreover, identifying any remaining undetected threats is crucial."

This approach to risk management enables the team not only to track work progress but also to actively respond to changing circumstances, thereby reducing the negative impact of potential risks.

Risk management in Agile is not a static process. It requires constant attention, adaptation, and feedback from the team. However, thanks to its flexibility and focus on continuous improvement, Agile allows teams to effectively manage risks, even in the most unpredictable situations.

This dynamic approach ensures that risk management is an integral part of the Agile workflow, promoting a culture of proactive risk assessment and response. By integrating risk management into daily routines and decision-making processes, teams can better anticipate challenges and respond swiftly, maintaining the momentum and success of their projects even in the face of uncertainty and change.

Risk management in Agile works like a set of control indicators on a dashboard. If you have experience driving a car and are accustomed to the dashboard allowing you to monitor all the car's parameters, you'll appreciate managing projects through dashboards and cards.

A project information card should answer, among other things, the following questions:
- What problems does the team face?
- Who is the executor of the task?
- How many tasks are currently with the developers?
- What are the priorities of the tasks?

- Which tasks will be launched next?
- Which tasks are in progress and what are their dead-lines?
- Which tasks have been completed by the developers, and which are tested and implemented by the testers, etc.

RISKS FROM THE PERSPECTIVE OF DIFFERENT TEAM MEMBERS

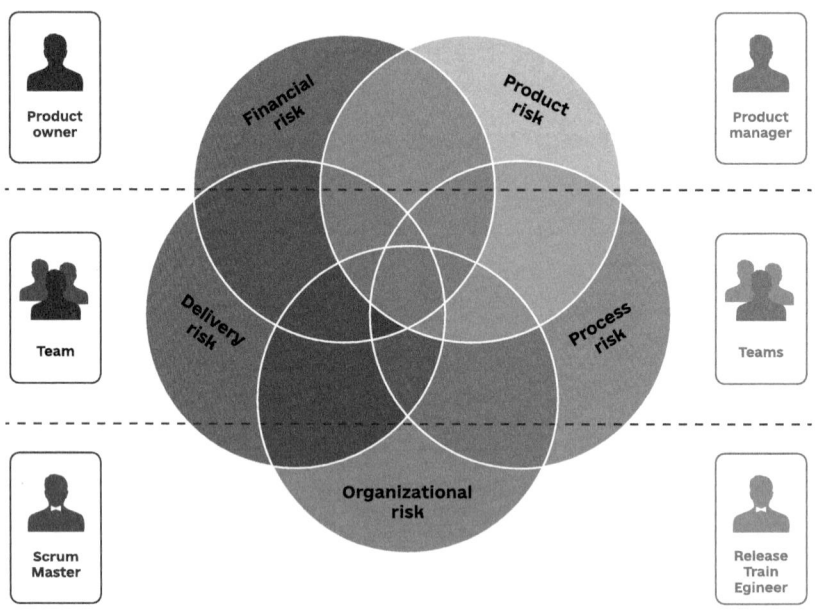

If there is a problem in the project, the team can see and correct it. In such a case, clients understand that everything is under control.

Are you geographically distant from your development team, or is it scattered across various locations? Do you face chaos, with unclear software requirements, yet need to initiate work? Is there a partial or complete funding deficiency? Is your team comprised of volunteers whose commitment is solely based on moral obligation?

Then Agile is the only way to work in such a complex and uncertain environment, where the main goal is to achieve a powerful result.

Agile's flexible framework adapts well to varying project demands and team dynamics. It allows teams to collaborate effectively, even when conditions are less than ideal, providing a structured yet adaptable approach to achieving project goals in the face of uncertainty.

> *As I sit in a dimly lit room, my young daughter, with her tender hands, applies a tourniquet to my arm. She has memorized the MARCH protocol, a knowledge most children her age should be spared of. It's a bitter-sweet moment, knowing that this experience might save lives, yet wishing she didn't have to bear such burdens.*
>
> *Risk has become our constant companion, an insepara-ble part of our lives. We've accepted the ultimate risk — to live, work, and fight in a country torn apart by war. We've adjusted to a life under constant missile strikes, the blaring sirens of air raid alerts becoming our nightly lullaby. But we don't ignore these risks. Like seasoned motorists, we monitor the indicators, adjusting our course when the lights turn red or yellow.*

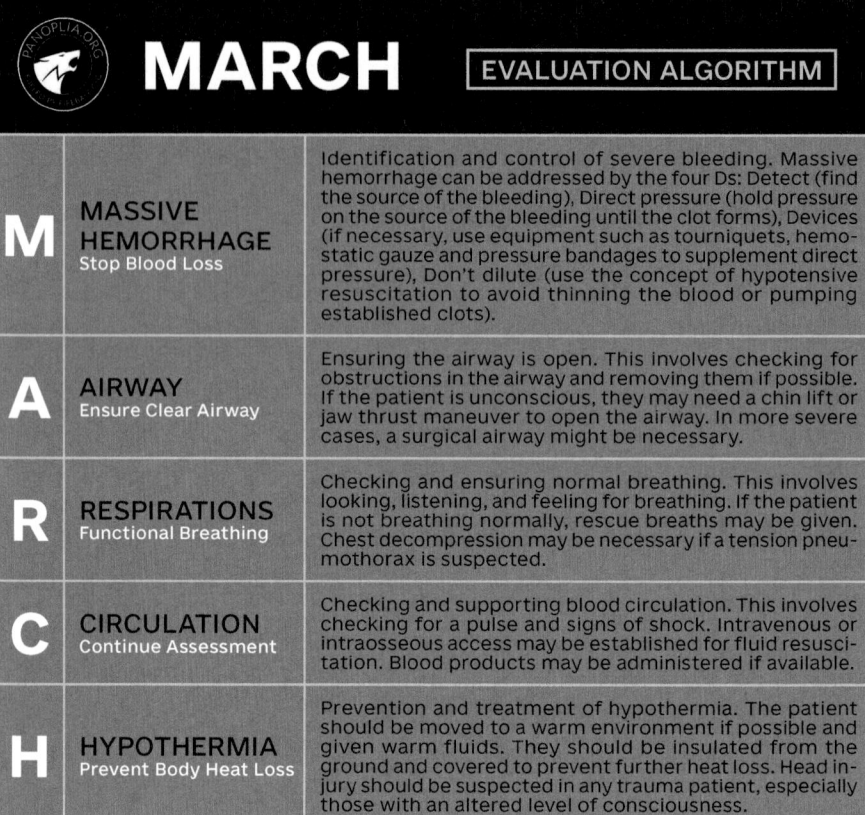

MARCH
EVALUATION ALGORITHM

M	**MASSIVE HEMORRHAGE** Stop Blood Loss	Identification and control of severe bleeding. Massive hemorrhage can be addressed by the four Ds: Detect (find the source of the bleeding), Direct pressure (hold pressure on the source of the bleeding until the clot forms), Devices (if necessary, use equipment such as tourniquets, hemostatic gauze and pressure bandages to supplement direct pressure), Don't dilute (use the concept of hypotensive resuscitation to avoid thinning the blood or pumping established clots).
A	**AIRWAY** Ensure Clear Airway	Ensuring the airway is open. This involves checking for obstructions in the airway and removing them if possible. If the patient is unconscious, they may need a chin lift or jaw thrust maneuver to open the airway. In more severe cases, a surgical airway might be necessary.
R	**RESPIRATIONS** Functional Breathing	Checking and ensuring normal breathing. This involves looking, listening, and feeling for breathing. If the patient is not breathing normally, rescue breaths may be given. Chest decompression may be necessary if a tension pneumothorax is suspected.
C	**CIRCULATION** Continue Assessment	Checking and supporting blood circulation. This involves checking for a pulse and signs of shock. Intravenous or intraosseous access may be established for fluid resuscitation. Blood products may be administered if available.
H	**HYPOTHERMIA** Prevent Body Heat Loss	Prevention and treatment of hypothermia. The patient should be moved to a warm environment if possible and given warm fluids. They should be insulated from the ground and covered to prevent further heat loss. Head injury should be suspected in any trauma patient, especially those with an altered level of consciousness.

2.3. The Role of Technology and Innovation in System Resilience

"The value of an idea lies in the using of it."

Thomas Edison

In the morning, in the back seat of a taxi on the way to the office, I traditionally review the main dashboards.

On these dashboards, you can get services that yesterday could only be obtained by personally contacting the social security authorities at your place of residence. And now they are available online and the numbers show that more and more people are applying online. Our work on these services is ongoing because some of them are still semi-automatic and require the supervision of social security officials.

But we are confidently moving towards the creation of automatic services and the first of them are already working. In such cases, decisions are instantly made based on transparent algorithms, which avoids the human factor and errors, and the state becomes more convenient and transparent for people.

In the throes of war, my role as a civilian leader has been defined by swift decision-making and the innovative use of cutting-edge technology. We are on a mission to make critical public services more efficient, transparent, and accessible. Our vision is to eliminate manual inefficiencies and errors, seamlessly transitioning towards automated services. Step by step, we are making the state more user-friendly for its people.

At the start of the war, thanks to the Ministry of Digital Transformation and Ajax, Ukrainians received an app. It told them about air raid alerts on their phones. The e-Enemy chatbot lets people report Russian military movements online in occupied cities. When there was no power or communication, Starlink kits with diesel generators gave fast internet access to the military, social services, and humanitarian teams.

The swift, unconventional use of tech also ensured that social aid payments continued. It included those who used to get help from now-occupied areas. Handling over 5 million displaced people was a big task, although new software and the Diia app, where people could register themselves, made it possible.

Around this time, the world found out about ChatGPT. We started using it, too, for practical tasks. It saved time, like having a personal team of invisible assistants.

You might be tempted to throw the book away, knowing this, but AI helped me write it. It didn't write the book for me,rather it acted like a coach. It suggested book formats, word counts, and even logic of the text. This was my first book; without the guidance, I'd have been lost.

Sometimes, I used it to argue with my thoughts. The quotes at the start of each chapter? It did those too, though I had to check them. It made up some "quotes" from famous people. However, I always chose the best options it gave me.

I drafted the book cover myself, using Midjourney. I spent ages picking prompts and images, but a designer finished it off.

If you don't like this way of automating writing, tell me on LinkedIn or Facebook. Let's talk about it. Without this help, I wouldn't have had time for the book.

Nevertheless, this chapter's not about tech in writing. It's about solutions that helped us act fast and big, keeping IT systems for Ukrainian social protection stable.

Two years before the war, we had the COVID-19 test. The tech and methods from then were useful in the war, too.

Remote services made things more accessible for people and cut state costs, but in the pandemic and war, they became vital for safety.

During the invasion, our commitment to making social assistance easily accessible led us to enhance the back-of-fice of social services. We leveraged the Diia app and portal, transforming them into a comprehensive one-stop shop for state serviceIn parallel, we developed the Unified Information System of the Social Sphere. This initiative enabled us to introduce several key services:

- Centralized registration and payment of housing assistance for over 5 million internally displaced persons, many of whom registered through Diia.
- An innovative system of online consultations and the registration of prospective parents for adoption of children.
- Four essential social aids for families, caregivers of sick children, individuals with disabilities, and single parents.

Just imagine how the implementation of such services has reduced the movement of hundreds of thousands of people between state institutions and relieved the state of operational burdens. In such services, there's a significant convergence of everyone's interests, resulting in a synergistic effect that alleviates bureaucratic pressure on society and adds robustness to the state, allowing it to focus efforts on other tasks.

Additionally, I want to talk about our team's creation of the electronic case management system for social services, developed entirely from scratch. This initiative marks a significant advancement in streamlining and modernizing the provision of social services. The transition to an electronic platform has greatly enhanced efficiency, transparency, and accessibility. This system not only simplifies the process for users but also enables the authorities to manage resources more effectively. Adopting electronic case management demonstrates our commitment to using technology for the public good. It transforms how social services are delivered and contributes to a more responsive and robust governmental framework.

Essentially, case management involves identifying an individual's problem, developing an action plan to solve it, coordinating resources and services to achieve the goal, and monitoring and evaluating the results. In social work, this translates to providing coordinated assistance and support to those in challenging life circumstances.

Electronic case management entails using computer processes at all stages, from needs analysis to result evaluation. All information about clients, their needs, plans, and outcomes are also stored in a single, secure electronic format.

The primary advantage of electronic case management is its efficiency, allowing a greater focus on directly supporting clients, as it can automate most administrative and organizational tasks.

Interestingly, while such technology is completely absent in Ukraine's social sector, it has been used in the private sector for decades. Private businesses, striving for competitiveness and efficiency, have long adopted these approaches in service businesses, banking, logistics. Our comparison of existing systems with our practices reaffirmed my belief that it's crucial for the government to outsource services as much as possible. Then, due to competition, there will be both high-quality service provision and optimal cost-efficiency.

An analysis of global experience has demonstrated that the implementing electronic case management for social services, which actively utilizes information technology, leads to improved outcomes. Instead of merely adopting this approach, we chose to develop a more comprehensive and automated solution. This solution leverages the capabilities of the Unified Information System of the social sphere, implemented by our team, and facilitates information exchanges with other ministries.

This approach not only streamlines the process but also ensures a more integrated and efficient service delivery. By leveraging the interconnectedness of various government entities and harnessing technology, we have been able to create a system that not only meets the current needs but is also scalable and adaptable for future demands. The integration of our system with other ministries allows for a seamless exchange of information, enhancing the effectiveness and accuracy of the services provided. This initiative marks a significant step forward in modernizing social service delivery, making it more accessible, user-friendly, and responsive to the needs of the public.

Consequently, we can assert that Ukraine is implementing electronic services and online platforms, which are becoming the standard for delivering quality social services and simplifying interactions between citizens and government bodies.

Moreover, this approach also creates opportunities for the development of the social services market, making it more attractive to the private sector due to its transparency and the ability to plan and calculate business models.

In addition to these planned initiatives, it's important to mention the one that wasn't planned but had the most significant impact in 2022, earning the team six international awards.

On the very first day of the war, we recognized the urgent need to quickly connect people in need with volunteers or benefactors for rapid humanitarian response. We started with a simple Google form and quickly realized we were not alone in this endeavor. The powerful spirit of unity among Ukrainians was immediately felt, as a vast number of state bodies and non-governmental organizations joined the effort.

This initiative exemplifies our team's remarkable adaptability and responsiveness to unexpected challenges, reflecting a deep commitment to serving the community and addressing urgent needs in times of crisis.

This "competition" did not deter us from building the system. The Ministry of Social Policy, according to its mandate, is responsible for forming and implementing state policy in the areas of social protection, volunteer activities, and is the specially authorized governmental body for providing humanitarian assistance.

In the initial phase, in March 2022, we implemented the ability for one party to submit a request for help, and for volunteers on the other side to find a person, learn about their needs, arrive at their location, and provide assistance. We designed this functionality to be made simple, clear, and reliable. After work, I tested it myself in my neighborhood, delivering food packages to people with disabilities, the elderly, and mothers with small children.

However, this functionality had a significant limitation: help could only be provided in person, in the city where you are located, or by mail, which was unreliable at the time.

This limitation inspired the team to be creative, and by April, we had implemented the possibility of online assistance. This system functioned like gift certificates for medicine, food, and fuel, which benefactors could purchase and transfer to those in need via a platform code in an SMS. The benefactor would receive an electronic receipt that listed the purchases from the store.

This was a novel experience for the team. We continued to refine and adjust the platform over time. Thanks to this innovation, people from 54 countries were able to join and help more than 40,000 families online.

The third function of the platform became the disbursement of financial aid to Ukrainians from UN agencies and charitable and humanitarian organizations. All these entities required verification of the recipients' social statuses, consent for the transfer of personal data, and, at that time, many even lacked accounts in Ukrainian banks.

Thanks to an application form synchronized with the Unified Social Register, we were able to meet all these requirements. Within four months, we processed over 10 million application, through which nearly 9 million Ukrainians received aid totaling almost 1 billion dollars.

Each organization provided aid to those categories of Ukrainians they chose, in the amount they could afford, using the payment instruments they had. As Denise Brown, the UN Coordinator in Ukraine, said, this was their first experience using national platforms for payments, and it turned out to be very successful.

This initiative demonstrated an innovative approach to leveraging technology for social good. It effectively linked international aid with national systems, ensuring efficient and transparent aid distribution. This serves as a model for future collaborations between national governments and international organizations in providing timely and targeted assistance to those in need.

Tristan Evans presents Kostiantyn Koshelenko with the Go Global Awards 2022 award from the International Trade Council in the category "Technological Innovation of the Year"

Now, in the second year of the war, we are reevaluating the platform, adapting to new technologies for supplementary payments to those in need. This allows international organizations to provide financial aid to citizens based not on a uniform amount, but in consideration of their existing income.

We are also planning to modernize the volunteer segment of the platform, essentially transforming it into a peer-to-peer charitable platform. This upgrade will include features necessary for organizations coordinating volunteers, as well as for volunteers who offer their time, experience, and physical efforts as assistance.

So, don't be surprised if you encounter more functionalities behind a QR code than what I've described.

https://edopomoga.gov.ua/en/

Some of our technology operates behind the scenes, yet it's vital for the efficiency and stability of our services and organizations.

This is especially true for the Unified Information System of the Social Sphere (UISSS), a project we have been developing since 2021, even amid the full-scale invasion. The objective of UISSS is to provide a straightforward and effective method for managing social assistance for citizens and delivering social services. It aligns with Ukraine's preference for online applications through the Diia app or portal, which consolidates all in-demand state services. Essentially, a system like UISSS is central to our efforts — a steadfast support in these difficult times.

Fundamentally, a system like the Unified Information Social Security System lays the groundwork for digitalizing processes across an entire sector. It represents a major project of infrastructural transformation comparable to building modern airports and roads.

Initially, we established the Unified Social Register to securely consolidate, in one central location, data on recipients of various types of social assistance and services. This register enabled us to establish information exchanges with other state registries, allowing our system to automatically access passport data, income information, and border crossing details, for instance, without requiring citizens to provide additional certifications and documents. This register has been instrumental in preventing duplicates, ensured data integrity, and has become a core component of the system.

Subsequently, we implemented subsystems for "social processing" and "treasury", as well as the payment component of the system. This allowed for the swift and transparent processing of social payments. Following the development of an administrative subsystem, we granted access to user-employees of social protection bodies and initiated the system's beta testing.

Another important system, which operates, so to speak, 'under the hood' but ensures the quality and effective scaling of services, is the national platform of registries, Diia.Engine. This innovative tool allows government bodies to conveniently and quickly create registries, automate services, and manage databases. With Diia.Engine, data can be orderly and securely stored in registries, facilitating the digitization and launch of online services.

"To receive a service in Diia, you just need to make a few clicks. But this is just the tip of the iceberg. Behind each service, there are registries and data exchanges between them. This is the foundation for creating a digital state. Diia. Engine is a tool that will allow the creation and management of registries. The development cost on the platform is half as much compared to the usual. The development time is 2-3 times faster. Currently, 50 registries are being developed on the Diia.Engine platform. Some of them are already operational, others are in development and will be ready soon," stated Mykhailo Fedorov, Deputy Prime Minister, Minister of Digital Transformation of Ukraine.

It is significant that building information exchanges between these registries is straightforward, facilitating 'data running' between different government bodies instead of burdening citizens with papers, certificates, and IDs.

Regarding the term 'register' used here, it refers to a comprehensive solution. This solution not only stores specific information but also provides electronic cabinets for citizens. Through these cabinets, citizens can submit information and receive status updates Additionally, they enable state employees to process citizen requests and perform tasks that have not yet been automated.

Currently, Ukraine hosts over 450 state registries with 80% being technologically outdated and vulnerable to cyberattacks. On the platform, one can not only create new registries but also technically rework and gradually transfer outdated ones. All changes are recorded and implemented strictly through business processes, which helps prevents illegal data changes and allows state employees to configure registries without involving external developers.

To facilitate the intensive development of new registries on the platform, training programs have been launched for its use by both state and commercial development teams. Our team seized this opportunity, gaining greater flexibility and capabilities. Consequently, we began building registries not only for ourselves but also for other ministries.

As you can see, a powerful, yet often invisible, digital infrastructure accelerates processes, enhances transparency and efficiency, ensures a high level of automation, and operates in turbo mode.

Is such an infrastructure essential for resilience, competitiveness, and customer orientation? Without a doubt, it's a must-have!

On the phone with Andrii Onistrat, who leads a squadron of combat UAVs (Unmanned Aerial Vehicles). He mentions that the military schedule is very convenient - when you wake up at five, you can accomplish a lot. We recall the book "The Miracle Morning" and share a laugh.

Andrii passionately discusses his role in the division's advancement, the procurement of new 'birds,' and the training of his personnel. While specifics are scant, it's clear that technology is revolutionizing warfare. It's heartening to know our contribution — supplying Mavics — is playing a small part in this pivotal shift.

**Andrii Onistrat with the received drones, which Kostiantyn
handed over from Andreas Keßler**

2.4. Impact on Management of Technologies of the Last Decade. Contributors' Conclusions

To gain a more comprehensive understanding of technology's role, I posed this question to several experts: ***"How have recent technological advancements reshaped your work strategies and methodologies?"***

Here are some compelling responses:

Derek Elder
CEO of Derson Capital

The evolution of cloud technologies in the last five years has been revolutionary. The assurance that data and resources are ubiquitously accessible negates the dependency on physical devices like laptops. This technological marvel has ushered businesses, including nations, into an era where agility, adaptability, and unhindered collaboration are not just virtues but norms, effectively liberating us from traditional office confines.

Jason Foodman
CEO, Entrepreneur, and U.S. Coast Guard Auxiliary Member with a 100-ton vessel captain's license

Managing organizations in many respects is about information and communication. Whether it be for training, sales, marketing, or support--a critical component for effectiveness is having fast and efficient access to information. CRMs and other collaboration tools, such as Slack, have made it faster and easier to store, retrieve, and use critical information about processes, customers, and the company.

Martin Vesper
Chief Digital Officer

The latest technology since 2018 that has affected work is AI, the automation of knowledge work, the automation of decision making (with risk assessment and profiles). This has especially increased complexity, and now we are working in a network of talents and organization that together provide a solution to a problem. So, we are working in partnerships, and even a so called "supplier" becomes more and more a partner with which we develop products or services.

Andreas Keßler
Investor and Business Consultant

For a long time, I worked with teams on site at the customer's premises. This has completely changed with better and better tools for remote collaboration, planning and development. COVID-19 has accelerated It. In my main area of work, the digitalization of business processes, I see the use of open/public APIs as a driver for innovation and efficiency: "to use" is better than "to build."

Haakon Rian Mansent Ueland

Social Worker,
Musician, and Author

With the rise of social media, we have seen a democratization of knowledge. There has never been a time when so much knowledge has been available to us all. But this leads to challenges. If you allow the perceived value of a wo/man — their financial, social, or inherited status - to sway you to their point of view rather than evaluate it as being another opinion, you are on a dangerous path.

Elon Musk has made good cars and rockets; the fortune he has amassed as a result of this doesn't make him a prophet. Therefore, curating and evaluating knowledge is just as crucial as accumulating it. Critical thinking is a superpower.

Marijn Markus

AI Lead Managing
Data Scientist

As a data scientist and consultant, the latest technologies are a core part of my work.

From the rise of Big Data in 2013 to the rise of GPU computing and Deep Learning.

To the resulting AI craze of black box forecasting, image recognition, misinformation, and deepfakes... to the Generative AI hypes of today, where transformers have become game changers in the ways we retrieve data and interface with search engines.

But back when I was studying it all, we simply called it 'machine learning' and 'statistics.'

Throughout it all, I've learned it is never about the new technological breakthroughs. It is about the legacy systems that keep holding the new things back. These legacy systems reminds us to not double down on new technology alone, but to address the systematic issues that keep holding the rest of the organization back--like old IT systems, flawed data, old work methods, or corruption.

It is inspiring to see how Ukraine is addressing all of these issues today.

Charles Mok

Visiting Scholar at the Global Digital Policy Incubator of the Cyber Policy Center at Stanford University

I have been in different roles as far as technology is con-cerned. I have been an early user of the Internet, first since 1982, more than 40 years ago. I was an early entrepreneur to help people get on the Internet, in the early 1990s. I became an Internet civil society advocate, from the early 2000s, when I started the Internet Society chapter in Hong Kong. And I became a lawmaker in 2012, representing information tech-nology in the Hong Kong legislature, until 2020. Now I work in academia trying to look at cyber policies and their global trends and impacts. So I tend to look at things from all sides. The closest that I would consider to be a war or catastrophic situation that I have encountered may be when China im-posed the National Security Law (NSL) over Hong Kong in 2020, Almost right away, the draconian law legitimized any interference and coercion China had been and would con-tinue to impose on Hong Kong. Civil society and any political opposition were completely decimated. Hong Kong's Internet freedom was turned upside down, from one of the freest in Asia to the most unfree.

All along I believe that, more important than adopting technologies and acquiring the technical knowhow, educating and developing the related literacy as to how to make use of the technical in a positive way is invariably more critical to the final success, and the sensitivity to appreciate how oftentimes such technologies may bring with them an unanticipated downside or side effects that we have to deal with, through technical design or regulations. It's a continuous balancing act.

Arnaud Contival
Civilian Leader, Chairman @AI&DATA

As an tech entrepreneur, with a specialty in AI and data, I've seen how much technology is a transformer for each individual, business or institution. These last 5 years, AI has accelerated and will offer great opportunities in all fields, civil and military.

Personally, I do regular tech trips to the US west coast to bring me a clear understanding of where main tech investments are going and which business fields will benefit from these investments in the coming years.

After massive investments in blockchain/cryptos, main tech investments are now going to AI and will bring lists of revolutions.

Chris C. Anderson
*Civilian Leader, Vice President,
Head of Content Division at GreenSlate*

I see the incredible technological progress of something like Ukraine's drone programs and see a future where Ukraine becomes the leader in defense contracting for drone manufacturing for allied states.

A.I. is such a massive disruptor that there's nothing that really even comes close. I'd compare it to the advent of electricity, flight, the automobile and the Internet.

I'd go so far as to say it's on par with the discovery of fire.

A.I., if embraced, has the power and potential to speed up Ukraine's recovery and drive the country to a brighter future sooner as opposed to later.

Mia Kolmodin
Civilian Leader, Founder and CEO of Dandy People

I would say mostly that what has changed at a high pace is that I collaborate more tightly with more people, meet with more people from any where in the world more often than I ever thought would be possible due to great online collaboration tools such as Zoom, Hangout, Miro, and Mural.

Mike Nichols
Managing director and Consultant

I have a positive approach to the latest technologies that have a positive effect on methods of work. Change should be positively embraced, however human nature and cultural behaviours often to resist change and this is the biggest challenge to change mind-set.

Approaches and methods of work, leadership etc, constantly evolve as technologies evolve together with many other factors, however in many cases caution is required as to the value and benefits for blindly adopting 'new' technologies.

Human nature is naturally attracted to Hi-tech complex technologies such as robotics', but often the simpler low-cost technology solutions are better.

People and the mindset of people are always the key factor of embracing new technologies and change. Different cultures also impact the change to adopt new or different methods of working through new technologies, for example the Japanese hierarchical culture often constrains the change to new methods of working.

I asked a similar question to my Ukrainian colleagues: *What new technologies and innovative solutions had the greatest impact on the company's efficiency?*

Ihor Smelianskyi

CEO of Ukrposhta

We are investing significant effort and resources into maximizing the automation of sorting and achieving 100% digitalization of the company. Our goal is to become completely paperless by 2024, through the use of devices, generator systems, and Starlinks, enabling us to operate under any circumstances in all of Ukraine's populated areas.

Hanna Bobino

Owner and Documentarian of micro-media YAKTYTAM

To expand our capabilities in producing diverse content, we are acquiring new equipment and mastering new media tools. For instance, using a panoramic camera, we capture the sites of shelling so that evacuated residents of Zaporizhzhia can recognize their homes even from thousands of kilometers away.

The documentary "Scars of Zaporizhzhia," about the October shelling of the city, has already been shown at the White House in Washington.

Artem Kovbel

Auditor and Co-Founder of Crowe Erfolg

We are currently implementing a new employee onboarding system based on artificial intelligence. For example, I can simply upload all the materials related to my product "Forensic," and the system autonomously creates training materials for the new employee. It not only dispenses these materials but also facilitates testing and evaluates the results.

Maryna Avdieieva

Founder and Managing Shareholder of "Arsenal Insurance"

During the war, the R&D department of our company has doubled in size, unlike other divisions. We have been actively digitalizing; nearly all our products were converted into electronic formats during the war. We are extensively using cloud technologies for data protection, IoT for insuring movable property, and computer vision technologies for damage assessment. We have even introduced AI for insurance assistance.

Yevhen Zaigraiev

*Chief Small and Medium Business Officer,
Board Member of PrivatBank*

The short list, though incomplete as it's truly impossible to describe everything, looks like this:
- *Google Meet, Zoom, Microsoft Teams.*
- *Online messengers and chats.*
- *Data transfer to the Cloud.*

- *A very high level of digitalization in products and services, eliminating the need for clients to visit branches for all basic needs.*
- *Omnichannel services, for instance, allowing cash withdrawal and account replenishment not only at branches but also at ATMs, information-service terminals, retail cash registers, and through POS terminals.*
- *Scoring models for credit decisions for microbusinesses and SMBs, introduced before the war and adapted during combat operations.*
- *Electronic digital signatures.*
- *And much more.*

PART 3.
Engagement and Scaling

Частина 3. Залучення та масштабування

3.1. 360 International Cooperation

> *"Coming together is a beginning,*
> *keeping together is progress, and*
> *working together is success"*
>
> **Henry Ford**

In the first months of the large-scale war in Kyiv, transportation was halted, and most grocery stores were closed. Those who were not afraid to move around the city tried to quickly reach the stores to get the essentials. Many people appeared around who couldn't do that and needed support.

Despite having a heavy workload, I couldn't ignore the requests of those in need on my way between the office and home. This entirely aligned with the approach of 'Think globally, act locally'. Among those people were personal acquaintances and those who left requests on the humanitarian platform eSupport, launched by our team. Those needs varied, mostly food, including scarce items at that time like baby food and medicines.

Initially, I did it with my own money, but then realized that we would have to endure for a long time, so it was necessary to work on providing sustainable support. In this direction, I also acted both locally and globally.

The greatest result was achieved thanks to the development of a system for direct payments to Ukrainians from international humanitarian organizations, with which partnership continued in developing digital infrastructure — the Unified Information System of the Social Sphere.

At the same time, the quickest result was facilitated by private donor Derek Elder, whom we met in April 2023. Thanks to Derek's swift response, we were able to provide hundreds of families with assistance, and importantly, a diesel generator was installed for the vital social payments server long before the winter attacks on the energy infrastructure. After a month of communicating via messengers, I was incredibly happy to personally embrace this brave new friend.

Another example of quick response was demonstrated in collaboration with an NGO. While huge organizations were only planning the deployment of missions, Hlib Kanievskyi, along with the Committee for Open Democracy, immediately engaged in assisting families with diapers, using the eSupport platform. These instances underscore the impact and importance of swift and collaborative responses in times of crisis, highlighting the vital role of both individual donors and NGOs in providing timely aid and support.

In the face of an overwhelming enemy, one that employs terrorist tactics by assaulting civilian domains and vital

infrastructures, the stark reality of our situation crystallizes. A direct, solo battle becomes an unsustainable endeavor.

In such dire circumstances, international collaboration emerges as the cornerstone of our resistance and the guiding light of our future triumph. Those brave souls are venturing into Ukraine on humanitarian missions or, as investors epitomize courage, discerning opportunities amid a landscape of risks. Still the question remains: how can we optimize our cooperation with them?

Creating a network of allies is not merely a numbers game. Quality takes precedence over quantity. The adage "The more partners you have, the more partners you have", though seemingly tautological, astutely underlines the importance of depth and substance in partnerships.

Success becomes even more rewarding when it's shared. Everyone seeks to align with a winner, creating a mutually beneficial situation. Yet, it's essential to acknowledge that failure is also a part of this landscape. When choosing allies, prioritize those who offer not just the promise of success but also show steadfastness — in challenging times, maintaining their integrity and dependability.

This book exemplifies this principle. Initially, engaging experts was notably more challenging than those who joined later, drawn by the book's established credibility and initial contributions. As the book neared its completion, a number of influential managers eagerly volunteered their intellectual insights.

It's vital to recognize the unique motivations of your partners. Their involvement is purpose-driven, seeking business opportunities, partnerships, or mission fulfillment. By supporting their goals, they become our most steadfast allies.

Providing insights into the local business environment and connecting with trustworthy partners are key. This knowledge facilitates quick adaptation for newcomers, promoting collaboration. In return, they offer access to global markets, cutting-edge technologies, or capital while seeking ways to offer mutual benefits.

Cultivating long-lasting relationships is invaluable. While single projects have value, long-term strategic partnerships provide ongoing advantages. Embrace all aspects of collaboration, including potential challenges.

The essence of successful international cooperation lies in its mutual benefits. Your objective should be to optimize its effectiveness and profitability for all parties.

When your values align with the global community, their support strengthens your resilience. It is achievable only through effective communication and engagement.

Your reasons for international involvement might vary in peaceful times, yet it always strengthens and diversifies your operations. Focus on this promising avenue by setting clear interaction goals, identifying your target audience, and determining the most effective communication methods.

Start with contacts who have already shown interest. Engaging with those who reach out first often leads to more successful interactions than initiating cold contacts.

Explore options like industry associations, exhibitions, and conferences. Engage with embassies and commerce chambers. Seek referrals from current partners. Consider launching projects aimed at international audiences, similar to our eAid humanitarian platform.

I firmly advocate for reciprocal partnerships. To achieve collective goals with partners and surpass expectations, methodically categorize and engage with them. This approach allows you to realistically evaluate the potential, timelines, and scope of various partnerships.

To fully leverage these partnerships, your team must understand the specific goals of partners, their committed resources, operational norms, expectations from you, and preferred communication methods.

As a civilian leader in a war zone, I've had to constantly evaluate my alliances. It's a delicate balance of power and a commitment to survival. Short- and long-term objectives and the partners' resources, capabilities, and responsiveness must be considered, always keeping in mind the human element in these relationships.

In this challenging environment, discerning the genuine interest of partners is vital. Are they motivated to achieve results beyond just fulfilling obligations? We didn't have the luxury of dismissing disinterested partners. Instead, we engaged more closely with them, involving other stakeholders and escalating issues when necessary.

Don't limit yourself to traditional approaches — be creative! For instance, getting to know representatives of NAFO allowed me to spread ideas and garner more support when I became one of them, receiving my own branded Shiba Inu avatar. NAFO (North Atlantic Fella Organization) is an online group of like-minded people fighting Russian misinformation and raising funds to support the Ukrainian Armed Forces. They do it unconventionally — by posting memes that highlight the Ukrainian perspective or mock Russia and its military plans. However, their approach is characterized by shitposting — using satirical and humorous content that sparks active discussions and reactions.

The group participants are not only trolling and meme enthusiasts but also Ukraine sympathizers. The posts about NAFO have been shared by Ivanna Stradner, a Washington analyst and Russian propaganda expert; Congressman Adam Kinzinger, an advisor to the Foundation for Defense of Democracies; Patrick J. Donahoe, U.S. Army Major General; Jack McCain (Senator John McCain's son), U.S. Navy helicopter pilot; and even Toomas Hendrik Ilves, a former Estonian President. Among the Ukrainians, who joined the ranks of NAFO fellows, were such government officials as Mykhailo Fedorov, Deputy Prime Minister; Oleksii Reznikov, Defense Minister; Vasyl Miroshnichenko, Ukrainian Ambassador to Australia, and other active figures in the former Twitter community.

NAFO-fellow's avatar Koshelenko on the background of the logo of the humanitarian platform eHelp

At some point, you may find that you are very active and have a large number of negotiations that are difficult to manage. Sort them out based on priority, potential impact, and the necessary timeframe for results. Quickly harvest the "ripe fruits" of faster and more realistic collaborations, which will allow you to stay in the game longer while calmly working on long-term interaction projects.

Social networks add a significant advantage to communication. My experience has shown that it's not Facebook or Instagram, where algorithms somehow favor the localization of a 'bubble' of communication and new contacts, but rather LinkedIn and Twitter.

LinkedIn has proven to be an excellent way to expand your international network. Here you can find and communicate with professionals from all over the world, who will help you develop your professional connections. This network is populated by people who are striving for success and continually learning.

Creating valuable connections is a key aspect of using LinkedIn. You will be able to build collaboration and exchange knowledge with people who have similar interests and goals. LinkedIn also helps you develop skills and competencies. You can find various resources that will help you improve in your field of activity.

LinkedIn is an opportunity to build an international network and find new opportunities for your own development and the development of your projects.

At the time, we seized this opportunity — thanks to a chain of contacts, Mark Ruffalo tweeted about the eSupport platform, instantly informing thousands of people around the world about it.

Among foreigners who come to Ukraine, one can recognize several unique profiles. For example, there are individuals resembling Indiana Jones — eternal adventurers who are always ready for challenges. These people are not afraid of the unknown and are always in search of new opportunities.

Their charisma, curiosity, and willingness to take risks become assets for the country in difficult times.

However, alongside the adventurers, other heroes work in Ukraine. Peacekeepers come with humanitarian missions aimed at saving lives and improving living conditions. They are endowed with great faith in humanity and a desire to bring peace.

Mark Ruffalo tweeted about the eSupport platform

There are also strategists, individuals who have accumulated vast experience in managing crisis situations. They know how to create long-term plans to stabilize the economy and society, see threats on the horizon, and identify opportunities.

Innovators who come to us with new technologies or ideas should not be overlooked. Their approach is based on the belief that a crisis is also a window of opportunity for growth and innovation.

Every business interaction has its nuances, depending on personal experience, challenges, and success stories. However, there are universally accepted strategies that can guide you on the right path in dealing with partners:

- Assigning an account manager to a specific partner creates an additional level of communication. However, personal contact at a higher level remains irreplaceable — it can be formal or informal, but always aimed at maintaining trust and understanding. Maintain constant communication. Find the optimal format for interaction, whether it be daily online meetings, systematic weekly reports, or a combination of both.
- The Win-Win strategy. In your relationships with partners, always strive for a situation where both sides win. This can be achieved by understanding the partner's needs, their strategic goals, and what motivates them. This approach promotes long-term cooperation and mutual trust.
- If your partner is from another country or cultural background, spend time learning about their cultural customs. This not only enhances mutual understanding but also helps avoid misunderstandings.
- Share risks. A true partnership implies joint responsibility. Consider opportunities for co-financing projects or risk-sharing. When you share risks, you also share responsibility for success.

- To always be one step ahead of competitors, try to stay abreast of the latest technologies and innovations in your industry. Your partners may have access to technologies or solutions that you do not have. Mutual knowledge exchange can be beneficial for both parties.

In war conditions, international cooperation is significant. Relationships anchored in trust, understanding, and solidarity form our bulwark. Partners collaborating during conflicts display commendable perseverance and focus. Their bravery, and our local insights, lead to innovative solutions to challenges.

By nurturing these international relationships, we not only bolster our standing but also engage in valuable knowledge and support exchange, discovering new strategic paths for development undeterred by external adversities. These robust international partnerships are the bedrock of our endurance and optimism.

Reflecting on international interaction, I can't help but recall one of the most important meetings during that period, and for me it was the meeting with David Thomas.

My imperfect English did not prevent us from understanding each other on issues of digital transformation of the social sphere and technological humanitarian response. Working at the World Food Programme of the United Nations, David had experience in implementing new technologies as an innovation manager.

With simple gestures and a quickly made and translated presentation, we examined the needs for developing our new Unified Information System of the Social Sphere, block by block, understanding the functions without superfluous words.

Later on, this system allowed our partners from various international organizations and UN agencies to quickly and directly make payments to vulnerable categories of Ukrainians through the platform eSupport that we created. More than 8 million people received assistance.

Kostiantyn Koshelenko with Matthew Hollinworth and David Thomas from the UN World Food Program at the 2023 Kyiv Half Marathon

Our partners also comprehensively supported the development of digitization, enabling the creation of convenient and effective services for Ukrainians. It was achieved despite the complete absence of budgetary funding, which had been reallocated to military needs.

When we ran together in the Kyiv Half Marathon in the spring of 2023, it was evident that we were fully aligned in friendship and cooperation around common goals and values.

I am also pleased with the fact that we are approaching international cooperation by learning English — the language of international communication. And now, it becomes mandatory for us, the officials.

On June 28 (on Constitution Day), 2023, the President of Ukraine — introduced the relevant bill. The law will now require proficiency in English for those applying for positions:

- *State service of category "A";*
- *State service of categories "B" and "C", the list of which is established by the Cabinet of Ministers;*
- *Heads of local state administrations and their deputies;*
- *Military officers serving under contract;*
- *Police officers of the middle and higher rank of the National Police, heads in other law enforcement agencies and civil protection services;*
- *Prosecutors;*
- *Customs and tax authorities employees;*
- *Heads of state-owned enterprises.*

3.2. Involving Volunteers and the Community

> *The best way to find yourself is to*
> *lose yourself in the service of others.*
>
> **Mahatma Gandhi**

April 2022. Morning. Bucha. My car is filled with Easter bread — the trunk, the back seats, and the passenger seat next to me as well. We unload them at the humanitarian aid distribution centers and then move on to Horenka and Moshchun to personally deliver to people who are still recovering from the temporary occupation of the territory and the horrors that occurred there.

We are in several cars, and all this is the initiative of Anastasiia "Stacey" Boshko, director of the Ukrainian Corporate Governance Academy, who has collected donations for this cargo among the academy's alumni in just one day.

During the war, there are no holidays or weekends, but when a few hours appear and you can switch from work to something else, volunteering is the best way to spend your time.

This is already my second trip to the north of Kyiv region after its liberation — the first time my car was filled just as much, but with common bread. Those were the first days when civilians were allowed in, and I took the opportunity to join the trip of Ivan Lukeria, Deputy Minister of Regional Development. This bread was purchased not only with my money. The day before the trip, I talked about it on LinkedIn, and several people from different countries decided to virtually join me.

In everyday life, the payment of social assistance and pensions is perceived by people as a natural phenomenon. The sun rises every morning and sets every evening, and these payments, which before the war were the largest item of expenditure in the state budget, regularly find their way into the accounts of those who receive them.

People are simply unaware of the number of processes and systems that are "under the hood" of their usual actions, but the first days of the war clearly showed that they are an indicator of whether the state is functioning and standing firm.

In the first days of the full-scale war, my team and I were immersed 24/7 in ensuring the stability of these processes and the first wartime payments. Having secured this, we began to delve deeper into the development of humanitarian response processes and faced a catastrophic shortage of resources and experts for their implementation.

At this point, volunteers came to our aid, some of whom were ready to program on a trial basis, while others helped people in need with their hands and resources.

These were people from Ukraine and various countries around the world who proactively wanted to join. Thus, we built the humanitarian platform eSupport, which allowed us to combine the efforts of the state, international organizations, and private volunteers from around the world in one place.

Volunteers are a formidable force, stepping in during crises to offer invaluable assistance without seeking compensation. However, as leaders, we must recognize that the impact of volunteering depends significantly on its organization and support.

Setting clear expectations with volunteers from the beginning is imperative. It includes defining their time commitment, whether it's a few hours weekly, a specific project, or long-term involvement. Open communication is key to successful collaboration, reducing the likelihood of future misunderstandings.

Though volunteers may not ask for much, acknowledging their contributions is vital. Expressions of gratitude, public recognition, or opportunities for growth within the project can powerfully motivate continued involvement.

Establishing a robust communication process and reporting structure is essential. Regular meetings, online reporting, and feedback channels can effectively track progress and facilitate timely adjustments.

Trust is paramount; entrusting volunteers with responsibilities in projects or activities can increase their motivation and commitment.

Finally, integrating volunteers into company training sessions or masterclasses not only enhances their skills but also cultivates a sense of belonging and camaraderie within the team.

Effective volunteer management is essential for maintaining stability and success under challenging conditions. Each volunteer represents a bridge to the public and the international community, embodying trust and support in a conflict-ridden world.

Rising from the ruins of destruction, I have observed the unstoppable force of volunteerism. Volunteers from within and outside our borders have become a cornerstone of our survival tactics amid the havoc and uncertainty. They are the vital pulse of our steadfast community, their altruistic deeds shining as a ray of hope in our darkest moments.

LIFELINE PULSE: ENGAGING VOLUNTEERS AND THE PUBLIC

IDENTIFY NEEDS:
- Outline clear roles and tasks for volunteers.
- Specify areas where public contributions can be impactful.

SEARCH AND ENGAGEMENT:
- Utilize networking platforms to reach potential volunteers.
- Engage through social media, events, and seminars.

ORIENTATION AND TRAINING:
- Introduce the situation and organizational culture.
- Conduct training seminars for specific tasks.

MOTIVATION AND SUPPORT:
- Express gratitude and recognize their work.
- Provide the necessary resources and tools.

INTERACTION WITH THE PUBLIC:
- Organize regular meetings and discussions.
- Encourage public contributions and provide feedback.

EVALUATION AND REPORTING:
- Monitor volunteer performance.
- Provide regular updates on project progress.

In times of peace, volunteerism may appear at odds with commercial interests. Yet, through the prism of social entrepreneurship, its value is unmistakable. Companies focusing on social good and integrating volunteers into their workflow can achieve significant advantages. Prime examples include eco-conscious businesses hiring people with disabilities or restaurants operated by individuals who have overcome severe adversities, such as homelessness or addiction. Volunteers are a vital link, connecting businesses with these special groups promoting empathy and collaboration.

For top managers, it's fundamental to recognize the immense value volunteers bring to the table. Their diverse experiences, fresh perspectives, and innovative ideas can catalyze strategic changes and drive long-term growth. Therefore, volunteerism should not be relegated as a temporary solution but recognized as a strategic resource pivotal to the organization's sustainability and success.

Running on Trukhaniv Island, covering my 42 kilometers of marathon distance, regular training and participating in competitions for me is not just a way to stay in shape, but also a way to energize for intense work. Every step forward is bolstered by encouraging words, friendly smiles, and the help of volunteers who came here to support the runners.

This inspires me to reflect on the contribution that volunteers, both Ukrainian and foreign, have made to the life of our country, especially in this difficult period, in this hellish marathon of war. People become an integral part of our lives, helping the country and society to work and develop regardless of circumstances.

I wish that the new electronic platform for volunteers we are working on will simplify the process of engaging incredible people in important projects. It should also help volunteers feel gratitude for their contribution, evaluate their activities, and interact with organizations.

As I run, I dream of seeing how, thanks to such a platform, the volunteer movement grows and develops. So that everyone who wants to help can easily find where

My journey began with retrieving my Twitter password and becoming an active LinkedIn user. These platforms soon blossomed into vital communication channels as my posts about life in Kyiv amassed a growing audience. Personal posts, like the heart-rending image of my children sleeping in an underground parking lot, proved to be especially impactful, resonating with thousands on LinkedIn.

My initial posts were sporadic, but I honed my focus over time. Inspired by Mykhailo Fedorov's example of how letters to international companies could halt their operations in Russia, I joined the fight. I targeted the banking sector alongside a team of volunteer translators, leveraging my expertise to elicit change. The results were slow but tangible as we influenced several corporate giants to make decisive moves.

When I learned that Russian military vehicles were equipped with European parts, I knew what to do. I penned official letters, included photographic evidence, and posted them on social media. My only shortfall was the lack of design skills to make a compelling post. Fortunately, Oleh Vdoviak, a top-tier social media specialist, swiftly responded with a striking image of a bloodied car and a call to stop. The post on LinkedIn garnered over 1.3 million views and elicited responses from heads of manufacturing companies.

The responses were cautious, suggesting ignorance about the end use of their products. Yet, within a week, under pressure from European journalists, these companies severed their trade ties with russia.

By April 2022, my letter campaign ceased as our actions morphed into a more organized effort. Diplomats from the Ministry of Foreign Affairs took the helm of international relations, allowing other departments to focus on specific tasks.

Ironically, what I was doing already had a name — guerrilla marketing. It was indeed a pure form of marketing without money but with a passionate team and a thirst for results. It was a different ball game when marketing had to be conducted from bomb shelters under the constant threat of bullets and missiles.

Guerrilla SMM – graphics about a russian armored car equipped with spare parts from European manufacturers

If you ever reacted to my posts, shared them, or relayed their message to friends, then congratulations — you became part of the virtual squadron of pro-Ukrainian partisans. It's an honor to stand with you against our formidable adversary!

When we launched the humanitarian platform eSupport, our goal was to unite the efforts of the state, international organizations, and global volunteers to support Ukrainians. Attracting international participants was a task unto itself, and working with volunteers presented its challenges. Yet, technology proved to be an invaluable ally.

You might think you're just reading a book, but it's also my way of reminding those who read the English edition about Ukraine, and to further activate and inspire those who read it in Ukrainian.

Is this marketing? Is it powerful and unifying? Can something similar be used to draw attention to your initiative? If you have answered 'yes' three times and plan to take this into account, I am pleased to think that this book has helped you, and I also hope that you will use it only for good causes.

By publishing this book, I aim to constantly remind, through its pages and beyond, that the struggle continues and your participation in it is critical.

For example, everyone can stop consuming products of companies that continue to operate in Russia. Additionally, one can make small donations for drones and humanitarian support of people.

Starting small, each of us can then more powerfully press in the chosen direction of the fight. Even with a limited budget, you can effectively influence social networks and offline companies that cooperate with the aggressor country, and by uniting with other people, create humanitarian missions and visit Kyiv with the cargo useful for civilians and the military.

We highly appreciate the support of each and every contribution, regardless of its volume, and will be grateful for it for the rest of our lives.

3.4. Management Practices and Expert Insights

I sought insights from top managers, both domestically and internationally, on their military experiences and their strategies for making critical decisions under challenging or conflict-ridden circumstances. Here are some responses:

Oksana Zholnovych

Minister of Social Policy of Ukraine

When moving quickly, there's no time to extensively test project decisions. Therefore, it's essential to listen to and consider different opinions about what we're working on. Because of this, various ministry directions are overseen not just by deputies but also by several advisors. Each of them forms a position on various issues, allowing us to see the problem from multiple angles. So, I always have several viewpoints on solving societal issues, and in making decisions, we consider all arguments. The speed is maintained because deputies and advisors begin to address the problem simultaneously and parallelly formulate solution proposals.

Non-standard approaches to solving specific problems are possible when the team comprises diverse individuals. Combining those with deep understanding in a particular area and specialists who haven't previously worked on the defined problem allows us to break stereotypes. In interaction, the team can view each situation detachedly — through the prism of those studying it for the first time and simultaneously considering the experience of experts in the researched field. From my experience, I can confidently say that if the goal is radical innovation and reform, specialists without a significant background in the changing industry are better suited for the task.

Oksana Zholnovych,
Minister of Social Policy of Ukraine

Therefore, my formula for management effectiveness during the war is the ability to combine seemingly contradictory approaches: speed and creativity, institutional memory and innovation, leadership and teamwork.

To maintain focus on strategic goals and not get bogged down in routine, we hold strategic sessions every three months, where during a day, in a space that excludes the influence of other factors, we work on our priorities and tasks. We also use this time to improve team relations and build a common vision for various processes.

And it's simply necessary to give everyone at least a day to immerse themselves in their own affairs and spend time with family and friends.

Such business interaction rules became a novelty in state management. Their combination helps to keep the team united and strengthen the resilience of each individual.

For me personally, it's crucial to remain efficient and find balance — to be amidst nature — in a park admiring flowers, walking through the forest, or playing with my beloved pets. It's also important to be sometimes in a place where I can be myself without any pretense, where I simply feel the unconditional love of those close to me. It always fills me with strength and peace. A special joy is also brought by walks with our dog Arni or spending time at a social ranch for rescued horses.

Victoriia Veremiienko

Partner and Marketing Director of Run Ukraine

Run Ukraine is the largest sports event organizer in Ukraine. On the very first day of the full-scale invasion, two key figures of the company: Dmytro Chernitskyi, the founder and CEO, and Ivan Tretiakov, the co-owner and organizational director, voluntarily joined the Armed Forces of Ukraine.

Any activity at the beginning of the full-scale invasion was out of the question. Frankly speaking, the company had no Plan B when this issue was raised in January 2022: what if...

Ivan then replied, "Then we close the office, take up arms, and go to defend the country." And that's exactly what happened. I am immensely proud of the sincerity and bravery of these people!

Ivan Tretyakov

Race Director of Run Ukraine

My first step was to join the armed forces. I began my service on February 25th in the reconnaissance battalion of the Air Assault Forces.

I chose a strategy to take responsibility for the lives of people close to me into my own hands.

In August 2022, I was transferred to serve in the Kyiv garrison, which allowed me to devote time to helping the Run Ukraine team. Therefore, the first decisions after February 24, 2022, were made by the team without my participation (and without the participation of CEO Dmytro Chernitskyi).

Martin Vesper
Chief Digital Officer

My military background is that was in the army during my mandatory military service time. Even though we were not involved in war we had tensions in our country during operation desert storm. I learned about how to deescalate in one way but to protect at the same time, something that is valuable in business as well, especially in change management.

The most extreme situation was the covid outbreak, where in our food producing business we had to adapt in days, using modern technology. It demonstrated that having well educated with a drive to get things done and motivated people in your company is of highest value in that moment.

The flexibility to adapt to unknown situations is where people are utmost powerful compared to machines.

Derek Elder
CEO of Derson Capital

I proudly served in the United States Marine Corps Reserves in the capacity of an enlisted infantryman. While my tenure did not include combat experiences, the ethos of leadership, resilience, discipline, meticulous planning, and adaptability instilled in me have been instrumental throughout my professional journey.

Particularly, with my keen interest in the Ukrainian business landscape, as ominous signs of conflict emerged, I found many around me skeptical about its actual onset. Drawing on my military background, I championed the importance of preparation to navigate unprecedented challenges, reiterating that businesses, akin to military units, must always be primed for unforeseen adversities.

Jason Foodman

*CEO and Entrepreneur, Member of
the U.S. Coast Guard Auxiliary with
a 100-ton Vessel Captain's License*

I did not serve in the military however I hold a 100-Ton Master License from the United States Coast Guard and am a member of the US Coast Guard Auxiliary. Time spent at sea has taught me to focus heavily on preparation, planning and training. Situations and conditions can change very quickly and that's when good training and thoughtful preparation often save the day.

In my personal career the single most disruptive event was the emergence of COVID. Virtually every aspect of business was changed overnight and with little warning. Most business communication had to happen online, trade shows were cancelled affecting how sales and networking transpired and customers businesses were shut down which had immediate revenue impact. My strategy was to stay focused, as they say in aviation, fly the plane. Specifically aviate, navigate and communicate. Aviate meant looking carefully at the business and impacts to the business (our customers) and our team so those could be addressed quickly. Navigate involved putting through into where things were heading and how to cross the chasm and overcome the obstacles (planning). Communicate meant letting our team and our customers know exactly what we were doing, when, how, where and generally keeping everyone focused and on the same page

Jan Dirk Geertsema

*Author, Consultant and Lecturer of the Course
"Leadership and Human Logic" at the University
of California and Kyiv-Mohyla Business School*

In an earlier career I was trained as an air force pilot. In this demanding career I learned to understand and embrace the importance of trust, respect, and professionalism. When flying in tight formation, you need to totally trust your wing(wo)man, and you do so, simply because you have no choice. If you waver, people get killed. You're all part of the same well-trained team pursuing the same goal. Trust, respect, and professionalism create a great bond, despite hierarchy and notwithstanding the diversity and idiosyncrasies within a team. I knew that I totally depended on my buddies, and I put my life in their hands the same way they put theirs in mine. There was no place for people who couldn't trust. There simply was no question about trust, nor about respect. Both were a given. I have incorporated this as a rock-hard principle in my leadership consulting and leadership development initiatives. The same that applies to the military applies to teams in the corporate world. (...and it clearly is why the Russians will lose the war).

Conflict resolution in the end boils down to finding sufficient points of common interest and agreement. This is where conflict resolution should be focused at. In practical sense, what I do with management teams is drawing a line on a white board. First, we write on the left-hand side where there is agreement, ruthlessly turning down attempts to focus on where there is disagreement. After completing that exercise, we write on the right-hand side where there still is disagreement. Usually the balance is 80% agreement, and 20% disagreement. This eventually will lead to substantial results. One remark: there is no point in finding agreement with people with cluster B personality disorders (read Putin). I would suggest to not go down that rabbithole.

Andreas Keßler

Investor and Business Consultant

At the age of 20, I did 15 months basic military service in the Bundeswehr as a radio operator in a tank battalion.

What I learnt:

1. It takes a lot of people to accomplish the mission of a tank crew, and it takes a lot of well-orchestrated steps and clear communication between all parties involved to get a proper result.

2. You have to trust others or it won't work, especially when it's a matter of life or death.

My conclusions were:

1. In daily business, the process is responsible for the result. Taking care of the processes is a key management task.

2. Build trust to people you work with. That's the basis.

Haakon Rian Mansent Ueland

Social Worker, Musician, and Author

Yes, I have been in the military. Since I have signed a vow of silence, I can't say much more about this, but I can share some of the lessons it taught me: You must trust your own judgment. Even in a hierarchical system, we must be responsible for our actions. Saying "I was ordered to do it" does not dismiss you from the consequences of your choices. It did not work during the Nürnberg process, it does not work today.

Alla Vanetsiants

Chairman of the Board of Pivdennyi Bank

Banks are part of the critical infrastructure, and these places increased responsibility on the leaders of the sector towards the population and enterprises. Initially, I had to strictly protect the team's atmosphere from manifestations and the growth of unproductive aggression with one hand, while with the other, I supported people, created safe working conditions, and focused the team's attention on the new work process.

It's unwise to run in different directions simultaneously; there's no point in focusing on a specific development scenario. It's better to act taking into account the current context and increase the company's flexibility and adaptability to external changes.

We eliminated most KPIs, rigid frameworks, and deadlines, and instead introduced softer OKRs, focusing on the meaning of what we do and the ability to quickly review planned activities to achieve the desired result. We gave managers more freedom in their areas of expertise.

Of course, I couldn't ignore the practice of project management in my book, so I asked experts for their opinion on the matter.

WHAT PROJECT MANAGEMENT METHODOLOGY DO YOU USE?

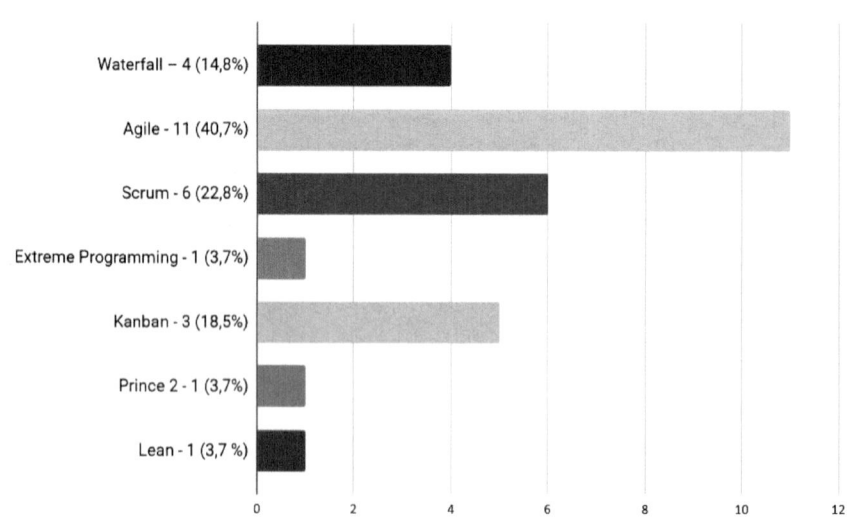

I am sure that my readers will also be interested in the range of answers to these questions.

WHAT'S THE PRIMARY CHALLENGE FOR MANAGEMENT DURING WARTIME?

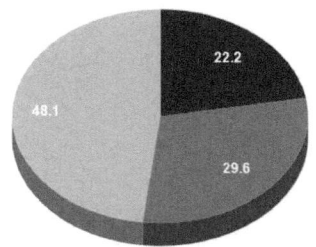

- Maintaining company culture and values (22.2%)
- Efficient resource allocation (29.6%)
- Keeping team morale and motivation high (48.1%)

WHICH STRATEGY IS BEST FOR A BUSINESS IN WAR CONDITIONS?

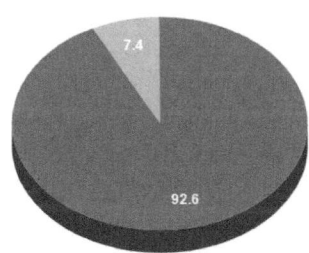

- Flexible: Continuously adapt to changing conditions (92,6%)
- Aggressive: Capitalize on new crisis-driven opportunities (7,4%)
- Conservative: save resources and wait (0%)

WHICH MANAGEMENT ASPECT BECOMES PIVOTAL IN WARTIME?

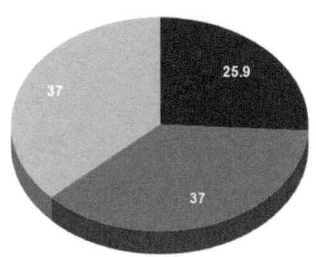

- Strategic foresight and planning (25.9%)
- Quick decision-making (37%)
- Emotional intelligence and team support (37%)

PART 4.
The Bedrock of Values
Частина 4. Фундамент

4.1. Learning and Development
When No One Has Time for it

> *"Education is the most powerful weapon*
> *which you can use to change the world"*
> ### Nelson Mandela

Before the full-scale invasion, I wanted to learn how to operate a drone to capture videos of the Dnipro and Khortytsia, Berdiansk and the Azov Sea, the Ukrainian steppe, and the roads my family traveled. This desire wasn't a priority at that time — I chose corporate governance courses instead, and only in August 2023 did I go to drone piloting courses with my son to acquire skills in aerial reconnaissance and dropping ammunition on the enemy.

It wasn't the only new military skill I acquired. In the spring of 2022, I ordered and bought my first carbine, a Ukrainian Tsvircoon S — a hunting version of STRIBOG SR9, which the seller praised as a convenient weapon not for trenches but for urban combat. It was relevant in March when I ordered it, and less so in May, when I mastered it, as the Armed Forces of Ukraine had driven the enemy out of the suburbs of Kyiv.

Before this, I had only held a Kalashnikov once in my life when we all made 3 shots at the shooting range at university. I was against keeping weapons at home, had a negative attitude towards hunting, and under other circumstances, I would never have bought it. However, in the first half of 2022, the carbine was at hand at home and often in the city backpack with which I traveled to the office.

Another new skill my entire family acquired was a course in first aid according to the Ukrainian equivalent of the NATO M.A.R.C.H. protocol, and we bought tourniquets to be able to help ourselves and those around us. I did not expect that my 8-year-old daughter would learn to apply it quickly and correctly in just an hour.

In the context of a business book, it's customary to talk about mastering different skills and competencies, but during force majeure situations, you may find unexpected needs for personal development and stepping out of your comfort zone. Even the term 'lifelong learning' sounds different during wartime, as you never know which learning experience might be your last.

The idea of pursuing education during wartime might seem illogical. It's hard to justify setting aside work or precious moments with loved ones for an online course or lecture. Stephen Covey, in his bestseller The 7 Habits of Highly Effective People®, talked about 'sharpening the saw'. In the context of war, it translates to honing the sword and strengthening the shield.

THE 7 HABITS OF HIGHLY EFFECTIVE PEOPLE

War brings with it the most effective form of learning: practice. Incorporating motivated individuals as interns, implementing mentorship programs, and fostering information exchange within teams turn project management into a shared learning experience. This approach allows for quick adaptability and team restructuring as needed. Participation in breakthrough projects serves a dual purpose: it facilitates learning while simultaneously achieving goals, offering vital motivation for those seeking development.

Reflecting on my days in business school, a clear pattern emerged; when owners and top managers underwent training, their teams often followed. It wasn't just about elevating the team's expertise; it was about speaking the same language and being on the same page.

In any team, aligning the level of knowledge and understanding is imperative. The central philosophy during extreme events, such as war or natural disaster, often revolves around survival. However, investing in training and development during these times is a key differentiator from competitors.

Recall a moment of despair when everything seemed lost. Now, imagine if you had additional skills, new knowledge, or a different perspective then. Would it have changed the outcome? This is why education during a crisis is not a luxury but a necessity. However, this education must be practical and integrated into our lives. For example, in the autumn of 2023, I had to decline valuable cybersecurity training for top managers because it was scheduled on weekday mornings. Such opportunities must be accessible outside core working hours, in the evenings or during weekends. I also missed most of a useful digitalization course because it was held during working hours on Fridays.

In such situations, well-organized distance education is invaluable. A prime example is the Diia.Education platform[6], overseen by Valeriia Ionan at the Ministry of Digital

---

6   Diia.
    Education

Transformation. It offers an interactive hub for learning and a wide range of courses that cater to the evolving needs of its users. Available in both Ukrainian and English, it's ideal for enhancing international competencies.

Engaging with outside experts and thought leaders is pivotal. Even if you are capable of teaching everything, it's not advisable to constantly do so. External experts, particularly well-known ones, can bring fresh perspectives and reinvigorate a team's learning experience. Inviting colleagues, familiar lecturers, and authors to share their knowledge can "level up" your team.

Creating a culture of continuous learning in an organization is more than a trend or a kind gesture. It's a commitment to improvement and a belief in the power of learning, even in the most challenging times. It can be the catalyst that transforms a terrible crisis into a future opportunity.

While on the topic of learning, it's also important to remember the need for a conducive environment for focus and concentration. It's impossible to learn amidst constant turmoil. Having fixed days or hours each week dedicated to learning is essential.

This is where our collective life hack, "Focus Friday," comes into play.

During a particularly intense period of work amidst martial law, we realized our workday had become an endless sequence of meetings, leaving only evenings for actual work. It was exhausting and unproductive. So, we experimented with a day free from meetings – initially Thursday, but then switched to Friday.

We stopped scheduling meetings, except for the most critical ones. This time was used for deep work on projects or one-on-one collaborations. And it worked. This approach can be implemented with the following strategies:

- Plan your "Focus Friday" in advance, identifying tasks that require your full attention. This helps stay focused and use time efficiently.
- Inform your team and clients about "Focus Friday" to set expectations and adjust requests accordingly.
- Turn off notifications and use technology to block distractions, ensuring maximum concentration.
- Be prepared for exceptions, as some urgent meetings or discussions may require your participation. It's important to balance focused work with team responsibilities.

"Focus Friday" is not just a method to enhance productivity; it's a powerful tool for cultivating an awareness of the value of time and space necessary for in-depth professional development and contributions to significant matters.

In our modern work rhythm, we often find ourselves caught in a loop of repetitive daily meetings that consume time meant for focused work on important tasks. With "Focus Friday," we aim to optimize the workflow, allowing for a more balanced and innovative approach to work.

Today is Saturday but we are together in the office. Yurii Konovalov, the director of the state enterprise "Information and Computing Center of the Ministry of Social Policy," volunteered to conduct a project management course for the team and share his experience.

Coming here was not mandatory for people from the ministry and the enterprise, but we have two groups studying here. In addition to knowledge and skills, we work on highly practical cases, as each of us plays similar roles in real projects in our weekly work.

It's also an opportunity to synchronize the conceptual apparatus and approaches of team members because among us there are people of different genders and nationalities, aged from 20 to 60. We want to implement joint projects as well and enjoyably as professional sports teams on the field and creative teams on the stage and behind the scenes.

4.2. War-Life Balance. Work and Life of a Manager

> *"I don't think of work as work and play as play. It's all living"*
>
> **Richard Branson**

During the war, there are no weekends or holidays if your work impacts the stability of the state and society, and you are genuinely motivated to make the maximum possible contribution. Days in the calendar cease to be distinguishable; the only difference is that during 'weekends,' you can work more alone and find time for your volunteer activities.

By the third month of continuous work, I realized that if I continued at this pace, I wouldn't last long. Even if I did, my efficiency, creativity, and perseverance wouldn't be what they need to be.

As a marathon runner, I know what it's like to go through long, challenging distances, but I faced such circumstances for the first time and lacked the discipline for a healthy lifestyle that would keep me in a resourceful state.

During all this time, I wasn't training, as I didn't have time, and I also had a foot injury, which I could only start treating in May when I had the chance to visit a rehabilitation specialist. My diet was also far from normal — coffee, a lot of sweets during the day, and semi-prepared meals in the evening. Working 7 days a week with a large number of varied urgent tasks also did not contribute to mental freshness and clarity.

So, I decided to engage in sports whenever I had the opportunity and started with table tennis, a game I had

In wartime, resources are limited and risks are high. People seek in their leaders stability, confidence, and clear guidance. When a manager suddenly appears with criticism or radical changes without a clear understanding of the team's needs and the local situation, it only increases stress and uncertainty.

War experience teaches us that leadership effectiveness depends on the ability to support the team, understand its needs, and be present and committed to the task. It's important to provide a sense of stability and direction to the team, rather than adding extra stress through unexpected and ill-considered decisions.

For a manager in crisis conditions, it's important not just to track strategic goals but also to care for the team, providing support, resources, and clear guidance. This approach not only maintains the team's morale but also enhances its productivity and ability to effectively respond to challenges.

Recognizing the reality behind the mask of illusions is fundamental for every leader. Remember "The Matrix" - we all recall the spectacular fight scenes, but have you ever thought about how it was done? Actors, suspended on wires, performed incredible stunts, later edited to show us the dazzling final product. The truth was simpler and simultaneously more complex: behind each movement there was a team, and behind each success there were numerous trials.

Similarly, business management requires the ability to see behind the scenes of outward success. Isn't this reminiscent of your employees working while we sleep, or the extra hours spent on strategy?

The portraits of Lesia Ukraiinka and Taras Shevchenko in my office, styled like "The Matrix," are not just a decor symbolizing digital transformation. They also remind us that every detail matters, even if it's not immediately visible.

So, when we talk about goals, strategies, or implementing changes, we must remember: beneath the smooth surface of the ice, there's always invisible work. This is a reminder not just to support but also to appreciate those who work so that we can glide. Recognizing this is the mark of a true leader, who not only manages but also sees with the heart.

Not everything in life
is as we see it

In such periods, you are likely to be working at least 12 to 14 hours a day, so when talking about balance, despite the desire to spend more time with family, the focus should primarily be on the office. Continuous work of such intensity won't be efficient — you'll lose concentration, become irritable, and get distracted.

Try practicing tactical disconnection and concentration — short periods when you step away from the relentless stream of information and decisions. Maybe you need to take a walk without your phone, spend a few minutes in silence, or even mark a moment when you allow yourself to feel joy or sorrow. It might seem counterintuitive in the world where every second is precious, but it's in these moments that you find clarity, which not only allows you to manage others better but also strengthens you as a leader.

Considering the psychological pressure and stress, it's important not to forget about the small joys of life, which can be a balm for the soul. Designate yourself some "disconnection time," even if it's just 15 minutes a day, when you can focus on something that genuinely interests or distracts you. It could be music, meditation, or even a short chat session with friends or family. Remember, even in the most challenging circumstances, you have the right to "oxygen" for your soulwhich will help you stay productive and focused.

Here are several recommendations for practicing "tactical disconnection":

- A brief period of physical activity, such as stretching or simply a few minutes of walking, can enhance your concentration and productivity. This simple act of moving away from your usual workspace can have a surprisingly refreshing effect on your mind.
- A few minutes of meditation or breathing exercises can be beneficial. These practices help reduce stress levels and improve mental focus, offering a serene moment in a hectic schedule.
- If a short evening with friends or family is not feasible, even an online interaction can positively impact your

mood. Engaging in light-hearted conversations or shared activities can uplift your spirits.

- Immerse yourself in a small creative project — perhaps write a poem, sketch a quick drawing, or even cook something new. Tactical disconnection can also be a creative endeavor, sparking innovative ideas and perspectives.
- Keeping a brief journal of thoughts, plans, or simple observations can be an excellent way to organize your thoughts and feel a certain level of control over your circumstances. Interestingly, such a journal might even evolve into a book in the future.
- Dedicate time to light reading, which allows you to distract yourself from current tasks. Choosing literature that is different from your usual picks can provide a refreshing mental break.
- Minutes spent learning or self-improvement can make you more knowledgeable and focused. This could be learning a new language, a personal development course, or just a short video lesson in your field of expertise.
- Use this time for a brief analysis of your activities, setting goals, or planning next steps. Reflecting on your achievements and outlining future objectives can provide clarity and motivation.
- Listen to a genre of music that you usually don't listen to. From classical to hardcore, new sounds can awaken new ideas and insights, offering a unique auditory experience.
- If possible, spend a few minutes outdoors, look at the sky, or simply listen to the sounds of nature through a window. These moments of connection with the natural world can be profoundly refreshing.

We live in the world of constant change, fast pace, and enormous loads. Therefore, understanding how to properly dose one's activity and recovery can be a key to effective leadership in modern conditions. By managing your energy and recovery as attentively as your strategy and team, you can stay at the top for a long time without burning out in the process.

I couldn't possibly overlook our contributors' perspectives on sports. Therefore, I present to you their insights— the secret weapon of twenty-one interviewed expert managers.

DO YOU EXERCISE REGULARLY?
WHAT SPORT DO YOU PREFER?

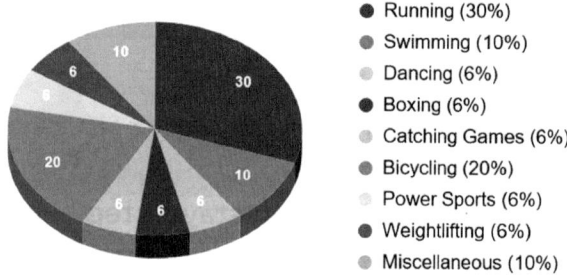

- Running (30%)
- Swimming (10%)
- Dancing (6%)
- Boxing (6%)
- Catching Games (6%)
- Bicycling (20%)
- Power Sports (6%)
- Weightlifting (6%)
- Miscellaneous (10%)

Sunday, September 10, 2023. It marks the midpoint of my journey in writing this book. My wife and I, along with dozens of others, are running towards Independence Square from the western part of Kyiv.

These nearly 13 kilometers represent the final stage of the charitable project Ultra4Ukraine. Ultramarathon runner Boas Kragtwijk from the Netherlands is running an astounding 2,500 kilometers over 50 days, from Amsterdam to Kyiv. What is his mission? To raise funds for those affected by the war in Ukraine. He also demonstrates how close the conflict zone is to Western Europe.

Boas' journey began on July 22nd in Amsterdam's Dam Square. His route winds through major cities, including Berlin and Warsaw, culminating in Kyiv's Independence Square. Averaging nearly 50 kilometers a day, he covers more than a full marathon daily.

I couldn't miss the opportunity to meet Boas in Kyiv. His initiative deeply resonated with me. It exemplifies how any one of us can challenge ourselves to draw society's attention to a pivotal cause and make a significant impact without massive financial investment. Boas has raised €66,887 for ambulances and medical equipment, but his contribution extends far beyond this amount. You'll understand this if you read about his initiative on social media and in the news.

Each of us can do something extraordinary to draw attention to a significant issue or to garner support. For some, it's running. For others, it's organizing charity concerts, writing a book, or knitting sweaters with tridents, like my wife, Olga. Everyone has the power to make a difference.

4.4. Personal Resilience in Turbulent Times. Alexia Michiels

> *"Everything can be taken from a man but one thing: the last of the human freedoms — to choose one's attitude in any given set of circumstances, to choose one's own way."*
>
> *Viktor Frankl*

The war and its consequences confront us with the unknown, which introduces unpredictability in all facets of life. Today's world and multiple crises (war in Ukraine, climate change, biodiversity crisis) are calls for resilience. Managerial responsibility and leadership skills must evolve and adjust to a VUCA context (volatile, uncertain, complex, and ambiguous). On the positive side, during the war, many people and organizations mobilize undervalued resources and demonstrate amazing resilience. It is humbling and good news for us all, and we should continue to build, activate, and strengthen our resilience muscles.

There are various theories of resilience. Type 1 resilience consists of mobilizing the necessary energies to find the status quo ante balance, while type 2 resilience comprises of initiating a process of transformation prompting the person, organization, or society to grow through hardship. Given the difficulties we face, it is clearly the latter perspective that I encourage leaders to consider. Growth emerges from pushing forward, bouncing back, overcoming obstacles, and leading with courage in times of crisis. This realization that we have to face and find a way through tough times is empowering and should help everyone make sense of their traumas.

come: the defeat of Fascism at the end of the Second World War and, some fifty years later, the demise of Communism symbolized by the fall of the Berlin Wall. These events paved the way for embracing free market economies as the key to joining the ranks of prosperous nations in the 21st century. Globalization had the added benefit of confirming the triumph of one cornerstone of US foreign policy, the export of democracy. The growing interconnectivity of both markets and trade also pushed countries toward a common set of presumptive democratic operating procedures.

US-Russia policy from the Clinton through the Obama administrations was forged on potential democratic partnerships and common geopolitical goals, a foundation of shared values that would appeal to the American voting public. Following the heady years after the fall of the Berlin Wall and Yeltsin's early democratic reforms, the pursuit of these policies became increasingly complex. Putin's FSB background and unmistakable authoritarian tendencies included the initiation of a series of reforms that weakened various branches of government, such as the Parliament (Duma) in favor of the Executive, election reforms that sidelined and eventually imprisoned the opposition (Khodorkovskyi and Navalnyi) and the nationalization of key industries to benefit Putin and key loyal allies to name a few. While a common language of democracy was sought, the US hedged its bets with an intensifying mitigation policy. This included a strategy of NATO expansion, albeit offset by US troop withdrawals, and a policy of supporting geopolitical pluralism in former Soviet Republics, notably in Azerbaijan, Uzbekistan, Kyrgyzstan — and Ukraine.

Putin started off as a reformer, presiding over an economic boom propelled by high oil prices. By 2012 and his third term in office, oil prices were under pressure and protests were underway in Russian cities across the country. Putin's goal was to stay in power. The promise of economic growth was supplanted by "militarized patriotism"[10]. It was also the response to a perceived siege on Russia from the West broadly and NATO specifically against which only Putin could safeguard the Russian people. In that context, reclaiming Ukraine for the preservation of Russia almost seemed inevitable. The door had been opened by both the invasion of Georgia in 2008 and the eventual annexation of the Crimea in 2014, test runs with abundant patience for the larger operation for the rest of Ukraine in February 2022. Victory in this war, in theory at least, would ensure Putin's larger goal of leader for life[11].

The debates about the final days of Yevgenii Prigozhin, leader of the mercenary Wagner group highlight a lack of consensus about Putin's strategy in Ukraine and the stability of his regime in order to inform/direct a Western response. Prigozhin's mutinous march on the Kremlin and the Kremlin's paradoxical response forgiving him, ending in the spectacular bombing of a plane in which he was a passenger, continues to puzzle western analysts. The Prigozhin episode is just one of several gaps in our understanding. At the start of the war, the US and its allies made assumptions that have not proven effective, especially with regard to sanctions. Specifically

---

10 Thomas Friedman quotes Leon Aron, "How Four Leaders are Turning the World Upside Down," The New York Times, 3 October 2023.

11 Thomas Graham, Monterey Institute Initiative on Russian Studies: Imagining Future US-Russian Relations (July, 2023). See also Thomas Graham, Getting Russia Right (New York: Polity) October 2023 for additional background on US-Russia policy.

targeting the oligarchs who have extracted untold wealth from Russia has not led to dissent, nor has it seemingly weakened either Putin or his resolve to continue his march through Ukraine.

Today, the historical perspective of autocratic leadership looms large in terms of how it might inform us both of Putin's goals and the swift resolution of this war. In that context, it is probably not a coincidence that there has been a flurry of publication of Hitler biographies notably by Ullrich, Longerich and Simms, all published in the past few years as the topic of Hitler's leadership comes into focus alongside the rise of 21st autocrats[12].

The brazen war in Ukraine is the largest land war in Europe since the Second World War. As each of these biographies note, Hitler was democratically elected in a democratic Weimar Republic. Once duly elected, he consolidated power within a period of six months after becoming Chancellor in 1933, and virtually unopposed, quickly unleashed a reign of terror.

'Making Germany great again' necessitated extending the physical territory of Germany, described as Lebensraum or more "living space" for the German people. The Nazis quickly marched through the Rhineland to Austria, annexed the Sudentenland, and invaded Poland, which sparked the war to

---

12 See Volker Ullrich, Hitler: Ascent 1889-1939 (New York: Knopf) 2016; Volker Ullrich, Hitler: Downfall 1939-1945 (New York: Knopf) 2020; Peter Longerich, Hitler: A Life (New York, Oxford University Press), 2019; and Brendan Simms, Hitler: A Global Biography (New York, Basic Books), 2019.

grow from a European conflict to a world war with the entry of Britain and, eventually, the US. However, the USSR was the main enemy, and like Napoleon over 150 years before, the Nazi incursion East to conquer Russia was the beginning of the end of Hitler's military success.

Regarding cause and effect, the new world order born in the destruction of the Second World War brought the beginning of the Cold War, a bipolar standoff between Western liberal democracies and Russia and the Eastern countries it had conquered. To many, the end of the war represented an opportunity for democracy, notably exported by America.

A return to the prescient writings of Hannah Arendt, herself a refugee from Nazi Germany, and The Origins of Totalitarianism (1951) recalls many of the eerily familiar assaults on democracy which ensued. From the vantage point of the conflict in Ukraine, Arendt's work reminds us how a series of tolerated "bad" norms results in a maelstrom of unforeseen evil. She drew on the example of the First World War and how it exposed the limits of national sovereignty by creating an unprecedented refugee crisis that challenged the tenets of basic human rights through statelessness: Claims of guarantees to basic human rights are meaningless unless there are effective institutions to safeguard those rights: the "right to have rights"[13]. Arendt also wrote about the relationship between truths and lies through the guise of calling truth an opinion, cementing the creation of a system of alternative facts from which the regime derives both legitimacy and

---

13 Hannah Arendt, The Origins of Totalitarianism (New York: Harcourt Inc., 1966) p.296.

power. One cornerstone of totalitarian regimes is that the boundary between truth and lies becomes indistinguishable and therefore no longer questioned.

Perhaps most presciently as Arendt's writings apply to the future of western support for Ukraine, a society marked by dissatisfaction and political polarization is also notable for its disconnection to traditional social structures. The discourse of the autocrat in today's world, Putin's baseless justifications for invading a sovereign nation on its border, draws our attention once again to the values that are at stake if we lose. Despite the many challenges Arendt describes that are wrought by a totalitarian regime, she remained an optimist, an optimism engendered by "the supreme capacity of man" whose enduring trait is renewal and rebirth[14].

Putin's authoritarian state effectively uses laws to "prevent" extremism to prosecute dissent. When does the Russian public collectively overcome its fear of punishment and turn on this "special operation?" Perhaps more urgently, Ukraine is relying on support of all kinds from Western liberal democracies, with clouds on the horizon. There are already breaks in the European resolve. A slim pro-Russia majority in recent Slovakian elections, upcoming elections in Poland that will determine the future of the Law and Order Party, dysfunction in the US government with the Far Right calling for an end to funding Ukraine are all emblematic of a brewing split in the alliance of steadfast support that the West must continue to offer as Ukraine forges ahead in the second year of this bloody conflict. A new war in Israel also plays in Putin's favor, complicating the future of aid to Ukraine.

14   Ibid. p. 479.

Perhaps most urgently, the 2024 US Presidential election presents a moment of reckoning, not just for the future of Ukraine, but for the future of Western liberal democracy and its values which have sustained the long post war period of peace and prosperity. If Russia succeeds in Ukraine, no country is safe from the aggressions of a neighbor. We can only hope that political leaders sustain a common endeavor to underscore the importance of this moment in defining the world going forward and shore up support. The march of Fascism during the 1930s was only defeated by a world war and genocide of untold horror.

Complacency in the face of waning interest in supporting Ukraine as this war grinds on is tantamount to complicity in imperiling the long, peaceful and prosperous run of Western liberal democracy. Faced with these challenges and competing priorities, we can only wonder what similar event is required today to galvanize public opinion to continue in solidarity to stop Putin's ambitions in Ukraine. This moment and this war, especially from a historical perspective, demands the same resolve as demonstrated nearly 80 years ago, which came at too high a cost.

In June 2023, on the bustling streets of Warsaw, I found myself in the heart of the vibrant celebration of Warsaw Pride. The air was thick with the spirit of freedom and equality, an invigorating testament to the resilience of the human spirit. Amidst the traditional festivities, Ukrainian flags fluttered proudly — a symbol of optimism for a peaceful, tolerant world.

We all deserve such a world.

Kostiantyn
at Warsaw Pride 2023

5.2. Conclusions and Principles of Turbulent Management. Roman Kuziuk

Freedom brings success.

Volodymyr Zelenskyy

Limits.

In our world, we are bound by limits.

Our actions are confined by the laws of physics: gravity, inertia, and cyclical processes.

Social structures also impose restrictions: geopolitical realities, historical backgrounds, national borders, and the constraints of moral and religious beliefs, as well as legal systems.

Even our biology sets boundaries: through physiological processes, illnesses, emotions, laziness, fatigue, doubts, physical impairments, and injuries, along with our memories and fears.

At first glance, it may appear discouraging. However, the silver lining is that every element, living or nonliving, faces its own constraints. As humans, we have the unique ability to not only exist within these limits but also to transcend them, achieving new levels of existence.

Manage to Think and Act Inside and Outside the Box!

People.

Every leader – whether a manager, CEO, mentor, father, coach, or in any other guiding role – should embrace Antoine de Saint-Exupéry's principle: "You become responsible, forever, for what you have tamed."

Conversely, especially now in Ukraine, it's important to remember a timeless truth: "One in the field is not a warrior."

The challenging aspect is that in tough situations, leaders often find themselves isolated in decision-making, and sometimes even in facing the outcomes. But the encouraging fact is that a leader is never truly alone, bolstered by a circle of like-minded individuals, partners, and a team. This ensures that in various life scenarios, they are never solitary.

If management is your chosen path, strive to balance the qualities of both introversion and extraversion.

Discipline.

Discipline is the moral and volitional backbone of a person.

It's shaped by numerous factors, predominantly motivation and willpower.

External motivation is not always present, and leaders typically have to find it within themselves, demanding a greater expenditure of mental energy.

Willpower hinges on a compelling answer to the question: "Why?"

The harsh reality is that willpower has limits. It operates within the lifespan of that very answer. Motivation, too, is fickle, fluctuating wildly like a rollercoaster. The uplifting news is that once habitual discipline evolves into a skill.

Nurture the Muscle of Discipline with Daily, Hourly Dedication!

Freedom.

Countless words have been dedicated to the concept of Freedom, a value we in Ukraine are fervently defending.

Paramount among freedoms is the Freedom of Choice. It has shaped your current reality: your financial status, health, family life, goal achievement, and personal success within your individual frame of reference (remember to be honest!).

To my fellow Ukrainians: We must continue our struggle for Freedom! To our international allies: Your support in our fight is crucial, for here in Ukraine lies the battleground for your Freedom.

Money.

Pecunia nervus belli — Money is the nerve of war (Latin).

Money acts as the lifeblood of our global order. Intriguingly, it's a concept of value only amongst humans.

Value people! Love them actively, creatively, and genuinely — this approach ensures lasting prosperity.

Technology.

Technology forms the essence of our future. Those involved with technology are, in essence, architects of humanity's tomorrow, not just in the literal sense of time. The Earth will continue its journey around the Sun for billions of years.

However, the "Tomorrow of Humanity" is sculpted by technological advancements and innovations.

Therefore, let your imagination soar! And remember: never hesitate to bring your fantasies to life!

Ukraine.
Our past is storied, our present is resilient, and our future is unwavering.

Glory to Ukraine! Glory to the Heroes!

5.3. About the next book we'll write together. Community on LinkedIn.

"The keys to life are running and reading. When you're running, there's a little person that talks to you and says, "Oh I'm tired. My lung's about to pop. I'm so hurt. There's no way I can possibly continue." You want to quit. If you learn how to defeat that person when you're running. You will how to not quit when things get hard in your life. For reading: there have been gazillions of people that have lived before all of us. There's no new problem you could have with your parents, with school, with a bully. There's no new problem that someone hasn't already had and written about it in a book."

Will Smith

Sunday, October 8, 2023, 7:00 AM. Roman and I are already seated at our laptops in my office, putting the final touches on the manuscript. It was his idea — to meet early in the morning and brainstorm, to ignite our synergy (because individually we are less effective than when we work together), and to "push through" on the project, especially since our deadline is on October 10!

We work diligently, and later, we will head to the new and modern ReadEat bookstore for the ceremonial signing of the Cooperation Agreement — essentially, an intention to turn this book into a bestseller. This moment represents more than just a business agreement; it's a symbol of our commitment and belief in the potential of our work. The excitement is palpable as we prepare to introduce our collaborative effort to the world, hopeful and determined to make an impactful mark in the literary landscape.

Our next collaborative book will be a journey we take together on Linkedin. As we navigate life, two tools serve us well — running and reading. Running trains us to overcome our inner voices that urge us to give up when faced with adversity. Reading, on the other hand, reminds us that whatever challenges we face, someone has already experienced, overcome, and written about them.

I've always held the conviction that books belong to readers' hands, not gathering dust on shelves. Good people invariably read good books, and spreading literature has a transformative effect on the world around us. For several years, I've championed a unique hobby initiative, the BigBookBank. Whenever I conclude a book, I share my thoughts on social media, then send the book to anyone in Ukraine who wants to read it. The only stipulation? They, in turn, send it on to the next reader, free of charge. While I'd love to expand this service globally, the prohibitive shipping costs sadly undermine the essence of book sharing. If you're in Ukraine, join the movement. I'd be delighted to send a book your way.

http://bigbookbank.online/

As you turn the pages of my book, each of you will take away something unique. Some may find fresh insights, others may rediscover forgotten truths, and some may question or add to what's written. But it's undeniable that every manager's experience is unique, and evolving circumstances add complexity to our roles. When you're constantly ruminating on optimizing your team and organization, it's only a matter of time before an article, post, or book on management is born. I invite you to delve into this book and join our managerial community on LinkedIn, where we can learn from each other and evolve.

https://www.linkedin.com/groups/9501126/

In this space, we're creating more than just a venue for feedback; it's an international platform for managers who aspire to discuss not only global and timeless issues but also to address the challenges we encounter daily. It's a place for sharing insights on collaboration and interaction, fostering a community where managerial expertise from various backgrounds can converge and thrive.

This book is unique in its structure — it's both holistic and fragmented, mirroring how I perceive the world amidst the conditions I faced while writing it. I understand this might be unconventional, and if so, I apologize. But this format opens up new vistas for continuing the narrative. As I concluded this book, I recognized that there are countless experts whose wisdom could enrich the content. Perhaps they'll contribute to future editions. This book is merely the start of a conversation. Never cease to seek new opportunities and chase your dreams with fellow visionaries. Remember, your potential is limitless.

Continue to learn and grow, for that is the cornerstone of success. Thank you for embarking on this journey with me, and I hope to meet you again in our next book. Until then, see you on the pages of LinkedIn!

Imagine the voice of Mark Hamill, reminiscent of the iconic Luke Skywalker from 'Star Wars', announcing from a smartphone: "Attention. The air alert is over. May the Force be with you." It not only injects positivity but also connects emotionally, as if the real Skywalker himself is speaking. In this war, numerous technological solutions have been implemented to aid people. These solutions provided speed and scalability, but those like Mark's voice in the 'Air Alert' app, with an empathetic and emotional core, were unparalleled.

The 'Empire of Evil', as modern Russia has portrayed itself, must be dismantled. To subdue it, we all must be committed to this cause and work tirelessly and effectively towards its realization. The civilized world must triumph and establish new security rules, allowing our children and grandchildren to devote themselves to development, not preparing for the next war.

Future managers at all levels must rise above their narrow zone of responsibility. Whether in business or government, at local and national levels, regardless of country or continent. We all should adopt a broader view and be more proactive in building leadership with like-minded individuals, focused on a happy future for people. This isn't just complementing the goals of sustainable development but is foundational, with the highest value at its core — the life and wellbeing of peaceful people and thwarting any cannibalistic ambitions that lead to genocides and the destruction of one group of people by another.

5.4. Post-War Reconstruction: Insights from Contributors

I posed a thought-provoking question about the future to other leaders: ***What strategies would you propose to Ukrainian businesspeople, top management, and officials to alleviate post-war repercussions or to operate effectively under such circumstances?***

Here are their most compelling responses:

Martin Vesper
Chief Digital Officer

I do not know the question, but I would like to add that if we look at our global challenges: climate change, the transition to sustainable business in the ecological boundaris, to provide food security, fight inequality, demographic change, all in a time where technology is providing advancement at a speed never experienced before, we have to build a strong network of those are on the good side, who want to make sure that humanity can survive and the future should be good for everybody.
I work for a company that founded during the second Industrial Revolution. We are again in one.

Arvydas Siaudvytis
Lithuanian-American Businessman

In truth, I believe we have much to learn from them. They don't require our advice, simply our support and understanding. I am astounded by the effectiveness and success with which the Ukrainian people, their Armed Forces, business, and government are operating amidst this war!

Derek Elder

CEO of Derson Capital

For Ukraine to truly flourish, its leaders must urgently transform the business ethic to align with global standards of accountability and transparency.

Mike Nichols

Managing Director and Consultant

My plan and aim is to eventually relocate from the UK to Ukraine and therefore I strongly feel a bond and connection with Ukraine and the people of Ukraine.

Preparation for post war is key, and I have seen many positives within the URC events I have attended and with discussions with my associates in Ukraine. A positive mind-set is a key factor. To take advantage of the situation to change and to introduce modern systems, solutions and management practices, use the situation to clean out the old Soviet style both physically and mentally (though I have already observed prior to the war excellent attitudes from my associates at SAUEZM and business connections with a strong positive motivation to change, to be innovative and entrepreneurial).

In my experience external support has and is always welcomed by Ukraine people and organisations (the issue has often been funding availability). My experience is that people of Ukraine organisations have always engaged with openness and with a genuine positive approach, but this has been constrained by funding availability and legacy Soviet style governance practices. A more fluid, streamlined and trans-parent governance processes need to be adopted, to take the learning and best practices from Western countries, no country is perfect, Ukraine has the opportunity to take the best elements to make the best systems.

However, this should also be with a cautionary observation with regard to the motivations of foreign organisations. Do the organisations have the skill sets required, or available solutions, do they want to partner with Ukraine organisations in a mutually beneficial agreement, is there a focus on the value of delivery of any partnership for the benefit of Ukraine and the people of Ukraine. Is there support with funding, commercial or international support organisations e.g. EBRD, EC or Crown Agents etc.

Jason Foodman,

CEO and Entrepreneur, member of the US Coast Guard auxiliary unit with a 100-ton vessel captain's license

We are essentially in unprecedented times, the first major land war (and all of its effects) in the lives of most business-men today. A common problem I hear a lot is, "I want to help but I don't know how". My assumption is many Ukrainian business-people, top managers and officials will feel that same sense of frustration, "We need help but we don't know where to get it". So the key is matching up those desires and my advice to doing so is network, network, network.

Get your message out as wide as possible using tools like LinkedIn, in particular the Groups on LinkedIn where those with common business interests can discuss, offer services and reach out for help. Governments are able to coordinate very directly but even they have organizations to (attempt to) help facilitate that coordination.

Small businessmen similarly have organizations, tools (websites) and groups, my advice is to put yourself, put your message, offer your services and seek partnerships in a very overt, direct way. There are people out there, online participating in various business sites, who want to help. They may not know where to look for you, what you have to offer or how to find you... find them and get your message to them. Don't be shy.

Jack McKissen

Author and Writer, a LinkedIn "Top Voice" on Management

In my experience, the people who cope best with catastrophe are the people who don't actually cope with it – who don't integrate it with the rest of their lives – but instead use it as the building block of an extraordinarily strong foundation.

Because after discovering this much steel inside your veins, what can't Ukraine build?

What can't Ukraine become?

What sort of extraordinary people and country can rise from something like this?

The perspective, strength, resilience, and grit that results from catastrophe is never worth the price you pay to get it – but Ukraine didn't choose to pay that price. Putin made the choice for you. Because of that, there is no shame in embracing your individual and collective trauma as the gift you never wanted – but the one you will use every bit of to make yourselves, your country, and the world better.

Jan Dirk Geertsema

Author, Consultant, and Lecturer of the Course "Leadership and Human Logic" at the University of California and Kyiv-Mohyla Business School

I am not sure whether one can ever mitigate the disastrous effects of war.

Instead, I would suggest that it is important to sincerely acknowledge the devastation, and start building from there, which should always first include conscious and deliberate efforts of healing at all levels. This is often forgotten: after both world wars in the 20th century this was largely ignored (society was rebuilt, but healing was absent), as well as it was after the Vietnam and Afghanistan/Iraq wars (veterans were left to their own devices).

Currently, psychological and physical health issues around veterans in the US (and the UK, Netherlands, Denmark, etc.) are causing great damage to the society, the effect of which is severely underrated. How Ukraine and Ukrainian institutions but also corporations handle this gigantic challenge will have a huge impact on the long-term healing of the economy and the society as a whole.

Andrea McKinney

*Vice Chair of the Hamilton
Health Sciences Board of Directors*

Continue to seek international support and investment, make sure the investment serves you. Be aware of debt colonialism.

Focus on tourism.

The Ukrainian people are an inspiration. Keep fighting. Stay strong. Thank you for your courage and resilience. Slava Ukraine!

Jeroen van Zelst

IT Director of Omring

In my opinion a balance should be found between a "command and control" approach and a generative management

Mia Kolmodin
Founder and CEO of Dandy People

Build networks with like minded people in Ukraine, but of course also abroad. Work cross borders, cross functional, multi disciplinary on short- and long term goals and deliver continuously.

What ever you can do to make it work, to make it just a little bit better, do it. How you prioritize your time as a leader is what matters. Prioritize action over planning and make sure your people get time to do the action they need to do. 80/20 is often a golden rule, and in war it is super important to always re-assess current state, take in new info and make decisions continuously and together my advice is to use the FICA model to do this. Make it easy for everyone following and networking with you to share your info and what you need — they can help by also getting others to support, because we want to.

People want to buy your services and many want to support your cause in more ways than you can imagine, because your cause is our cause.

Daiva Plath
Personal Transformation Coach for Leaders

In challenging times it is easy to let our minds be filled with doubt, worry and disbelief. It is these tough times that force you to step up and fully own your strength as a leader who can remind people of their power: The power to choose their attitude. It is in these hard times filled with fear and insecurity that your greatest responsibility as a leader is to focus on faith and hope. To give people relief. To bring light into darkness. To be an uplifter. Every single morning it is your job to decide that you will show up with love, compassion and kindness. That you will focus on your strength, stay present, calm and hopeful.

Ihor Smelianskyi
CEO of Ukrposhta

Maximum robotization and digitalization are key to remain adaptive and be ready to resume operations in de-occupied territories within a maximum of 2–3 days, sending a signal to the people there that Ukraine has returned.

Anastasiia Shevchenko
General Manager of "Lugera Ukraine"

Bringing Ukrainians Home.

The war has led to colossal disparities in our country's labor market. After departure, according to various estimates, between 9 to 12 million Ukrainians left. Excluding the non-working and unemployed, we have approximately 7 million working Ukrainians remaining. Naturally, this is far too few for the restoration of business operations and replenishing the tax portion of the budget, which is particularly necessary for funding the Armed Forces of Ukraine and implementing defense programs. Clearly, the recovery and rebuilding of Ukraine are impossible without the return of our citizens to full working life. All research conducted during the war on the key factors for Ukrainians returning home has shown: after the obvious answers of 'ending the war, safety for life,' employment issues immediately follow. The availability of jobs is extremely important for Ukrainians to rebuild and restore their lives amidst the realities of war and reintegrate into society. Employment or the guarantee of work and financial support for people have become key drivers of business survival during the war. Therefore, we decided to help the affected Ukrainians return to work and in mid-2023, we launched the 'Return Talents to Ukraine' program, to which we have already directed 1 million euros in the first stage.

Maryna Avdieieva
Founder and Managing Shareholder of "Arsenal Insurance"

We are already working on several serious challenges, the resolution of which will determine our future. Firstly, we are aligning our accounting and reporting, as well as our main operational processes, with the international standards of IFRS17. We believe that one of the main conditions for facilitating post-war development will be the access to foreign capital. In our case, it means attracting a foreign profile investor. If we are understandable to them not only in terms of our business model but also in terms of rules and procedures, our chances will be much greater.

Already today, we feel a shortage of qualified personnel, so we understand that our team is likely to gradually become international. We are studying the foreign labor market and paying attention to foreign specialists. A separate issue is the employment of veterans.

Victoriia Veremiienko
Partner and Marketing Director of Run Ukraine

Currently, every project created by Run Ukraine has a distinct social and charitable component: and it is not limited to raising money for weapons or medical aid. Our goal is to

involve military personnel, those undergoing rehabilitation, and children in each project.

When 13-year-old Yana Stepnenko (in April 2022, Yana and her family were caught in a shelling at the Kramatorsk railway station; Yana lost both legs, and her mother lost one limb) ran her first 100 meters on prosthetics during the Lviv Half Marathon – everyone around cried. That's when this incredible little girl said, "Today I am scared to run, but I want to support children who also lost their legs and can't run. I want them to see my act and tell themselves: 'Yes! I can do it too! I can run too!'"

Participant of the Lviv Half Marathon-2023:
Yana Stepanenko

In such moments, you realize that everything the team does matters. For heroes, it's to show their resilience and prove to themselves that they can. For others, it's an op-portunity to express gratitude and get energized with the spirit of strength.

I also want to mention discipline – it's like the backbone of a person. It holds you and helps you get out of any situation.

You don't need to look at others, their pace, as everyone has their own, just like in a marathon. The main thing is to see the goal and make at least one step towards it every day, and in 356 days, it will be a total of 356 steps in the right direction!

Dmytro Stryzhov

Founder of "Sheriff" Security Company, IRONMAN

The West has outpaced the rest of the world thanks to a cocktail of six factors, the first three being: Competition (limiting excessive regulation and government intervention. Regulatory authorities must stop being repressive or a source of huge earnings for their employees. The businessman is a fat goose); The Scientific Revolution (stimulating IT business, innovation, the state must invest in fundamental science); Rule of law, inviolability of private property, and representative governance. With all these, we are still in a sad situation.

Many of today's elite need to decide whether they are Ukrainians by passport, by the opportunity to earn, or by the call of the heart! Business will definitely not have an easy time in the near future! Ahead there is the war with the old system and the old elites. They will resist, as their previous state of affairs, where personal enrichment is possible, completely suits them!

Oksana Zholnovych

Minister of Social Policy of Ukraine

Some perceive the social sphere as working with poverty; whereas, others see it only as the country's second budget. For me, it is primarily about human empathy and mutual support. The war has emphasized that in the chaos of everything, the most important thing is when a person lives for another person.

Roman Kuziuk

Founder and CEO of the Business Literature Publishing House "Ultimate Beneficiary"

I've been impressed by the co-founders of Nova Poshta, for the work of Nova Poshta's contact center, which showed miracles of sensitivity, humanity, understanding, and inventiveness in various non-standard situations. I realize that the foundation of such a contact center is the company's co-founders. No, these are not just random nice, sensitive, and smart people who happened to be there; their presence, precisely such people, is the merit of the Founders.

I also intend to build a socially useful, efficient, and recognizable Brand, so I understand that I need to start with myself. It is necessary, on one hand, to reveal, and on the other hand, to develop a complex of productive volitional and intellectual qualities directly in myself. In other words, this is a story about habits and skills that can ensure stability, efficiency, and success.

Here are a few of them, personally mine:
1. *Formulating a personal life Mission. Its basis is my Dream – that by 2038, Ukraine becomes a superpower state, and I have made my modest contribution to it. The Mission is still being formed, by the way. But the basis is already there, so the movement towards it has actually started. In particular, for five years now, I have been publishing professional (e.i. useful) literature exclusively by Ukrainian authors. And this book by Kostiantyn is a worthy continuation of my cause.*

Then — breaking down the Mission into Goals and Tasks.

2. *Elements of discipline:*
   - *getting up every day at 5:55 without exceptions, weekends, or holidays. Every day. 5:55;*

- *fanatical fulfillment of the planned: planned something? Rest or sleep — after the last task is crossed out;*
- *sport-sport-sport. Previously judo, sambo, hand-to-hand combat, basketball, breakdancing, officer's decathlon, capoeira, car racing. More about this in my book 'The Sports Businessman.' Now: less running, more workout, occasionally tennis, swimming, dancing, weekly football.*

3. *Moral guidelines — without them, no way:*
- *from the beginning of the russian invasion in 2014, I immediately adopted two settings for myself. The first: absolutely zero tolerance for the smallest manifestations of corrupt actions in my country. The second: never under any circumstances switch to russian language with a conversation partner in Ukraine;*
- *the word of an honorable person becomes his obligation, this (still don't know, unfortunately or fortunately) is about me. Very often, this life setting looks like weakness and an unfavorable position, but at the end of the day, when you've kept your word — it's a wonderful feeling of respect for yourself;*
- *Ukraine — my country, I live here, grow, work, develop, and my further achievements — will continue to be for her, about her, with her... Realizing this adds strength at all stages.*

Yevhen Zaigraiev

Chief Small and Medium Business Officer,
Board Member of PrivatBank

Ukrainians are uniquely resistant to crises, only I had to experience the following major crises and disasters:

- *Accident at the Chernobyl NPP in 1986*
- *Global deficit, student revolution on granite 1988-1991*
- *The collapse of the USSR, 1991*
- *Economic crisis in Ukraine and hyperinflation, 1991–1994*
- *The financial crisis of 1998*
- *Orange Revolution, 2004*
- *The global financial crisis of 2008*
- *The Revolution of Dignity and Russia's annexation of Crimea, the beginning of the war in Donbass, 2014*
- *The epidemic of COVID-19, 2020-2021*
- *The full-scale war with Russia, which gained terrible momentum in 2022 and increasingly bears signs of genocide.*

So, we become naturally more resilient in difficult, sometimes extreme conditions and every crisis makes us stronger. For example, if we had not learned to work online due to the COVID epidemic, it would have been much more difficult for us to adapt business processes during the first weeks of the war.

We pay particular attention to the development and training of our staff. An important element of today's and post-war Ukraine is inclusion — we are primarily ready to hire veterans, people with disabilities, develop convenient products and services for them, lend business in de-occupied territories and business relocation within Ukraine, change branches, payment cards and applications etc.

One of the questions to our contributors concerned their opinion about Ukrainians who are abroad and will return home after the war. I was personally comforted by the results of the survey, as they testify to a firm belief that the majority of our fellow citizens will return to the Motherland.

DURING THE WAR, A LOT OF PEOPLE LEFT UKRAINE, WHAT PERCENTAGE OF THEM WILL REMAIN LIVING ABROAD?

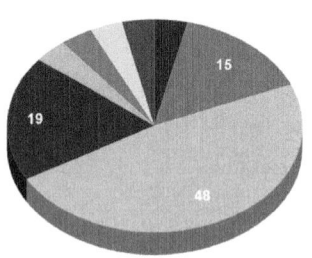

- 80 % (3.6%)
- 50 % (15 %)
- 30 % (48 %)
- 10 % (19 %)
- It depends on the decisions of the government of Ukraine, the average level of wages and other factors (3.6%)
- 2 % (3.6%)
- I'm not sure (3.6%)
- According to people I know, I would estimate from 10 to 20% (3.6%)

I was also interested in the answers to such questions.

WHAT IS YOUR CONTRIBUTION TO UKRAINE'S VICTORY?

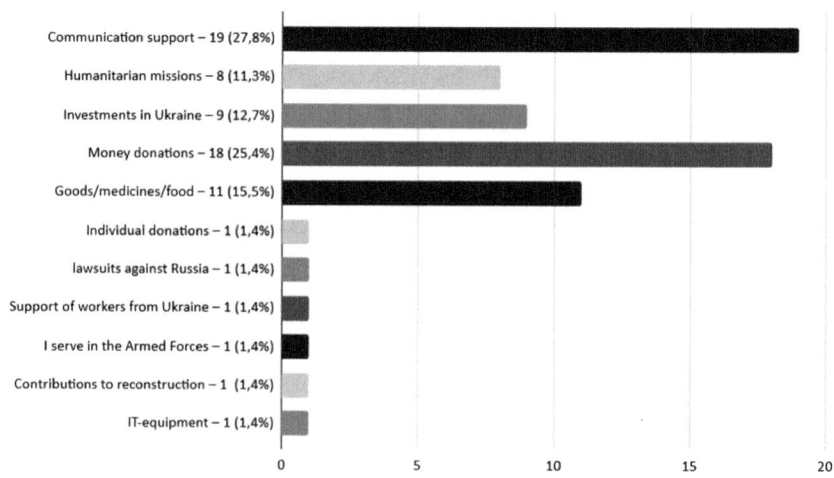

ARE YOU PLANNING TO VISIT UKRAINE?

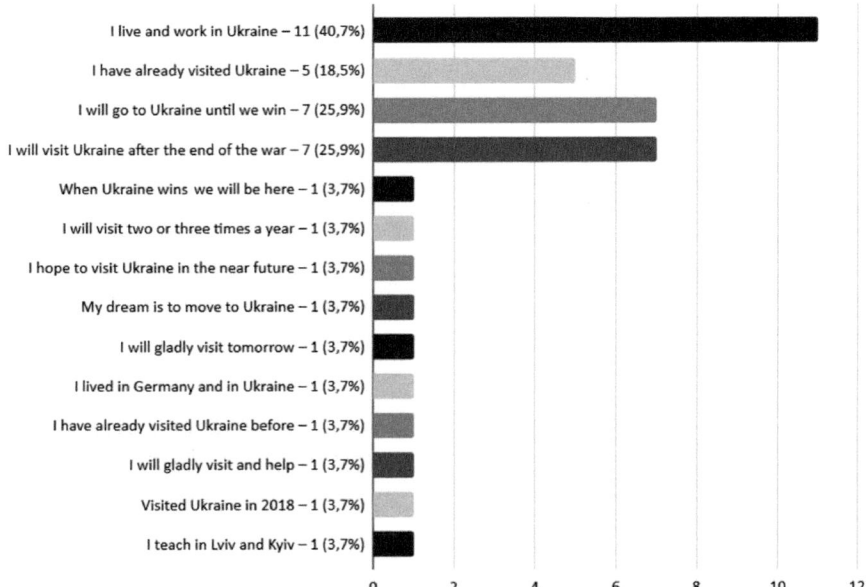

HOW I WROTE THIS BOOK.
A PERSONAL MINDSET
ЯК Я ПИСАВ ЦЮ КНИГУ. ПЕРСОНАЛЬНИЙ MINDSET

> *"Writing is a lonely job. And if you have someone who believes in you, that's a lot already. Those who believe don't need speeches. Their belief is enough."*
>
> **Stephen King**

"Management In Times of War" is my first book. To make it even more practical, I offer this chapter for those who have long planned to write a book but have not yet turned this intention into reality. I was like that myself for several years, certainly missing several opportunities to write great, useful books. However this time, the situation around us was such that Hollywood blockbusters would simply be uninteresting to watch. I could not miss this moment, and this book would not have been possible without a series of approaches, life hacks, and technological tricks that helped me achieve it. So, I will try to share my experience with you so that next year, you too may have your own book, or a substantial, useful article on a topic close to you.

I conceived this book as both educational and instructive, sometimes as an additional stimulus for action, and sometimes as a call to continue supporting Ukrainians in our struggle, reminding us that the war continues...

At some point along the way, I realized that I was inventing my own path as a way to create something unique, a source of knowledge and advice in the form of a book, which I very much hope will become valuable to the reader.

So, I decided to make a track record of this journey, because in life, it's not always just the result that's important – the process is valuable too, and a recorded, described, and documented process becomes a separate managerial product.

Great speakers inspire, but only your daily practice will turn you into an orator. Reading bestsellers is engaging, but only writing every day will help you pen a book.

I started with an IDEA.

It had clearly been forming over years and reached its peak just right now, precisely this month, a summer military month in the capital of indomitable Ukraine. The first component of my idea, shaped by my consciousness just now, is the necessity and my serious (and hopefully powerful in the future) contribution to the common cause of my country's victory.

A less significant but clearly primary part of the Idea was choosing the form to convey my knowledge, feelings, views, thoughts, and management experience. Therefore, the choice was clear — it had to be a Book. Not a series of articles in a popular publication, not a scientific work, but a Book, as an eternal, always relevant, and respected source of knowledge.

The THEME. This was also not an easy path of choice, raising questions about appropriateness, expertise, target audience, and timeliness of the material you're going to 'put into the ears' of your reader. So, my Idea about the Theme was such: 'Management During War'. Expertly - yes, because I have extensive experience in management. Timely? Unfortunately, that question is rhetorical...

The main material for the book is EXPERIENCE.

The experience laid out in this work, like most material in similar books, is both theoretical and practical. What is often missing in many similar works is the experience gained during war...

The literary tradition of stable expressions suggests my brain use the cliché: 'thanks to such experience...' But I immediately stop myself at this half-thought-half-reflex — GOD FORBID ANY OF THE AUTHORS OF SIMILAR BOOKS TO HAVE SUCH EXPERIENCE!

So, I sincerely share my gains with you, dear reader, as part of shaping your theoretical worldview in management... during war.

PEOPLE.

Early on, I thought it would be very good to provide other managers' advice and visions on various issues related to management during war in the book. Furthermore, within a week, Roman and I also decided to query foreign colleague-sand, of course, entrepreneurs with combat experience.

At some point, I ran out of energy and wanted to stop with what I had, put it aside until inspiration came. But that would have postponed the book indefinitely, so I decided to make a public promise. That day, a post about the book appeared on Facebook, which solved several tasks for me:

- The publication deadline became public, and therefore mandatory for me;
- Mentioning all the invited experts reminded them of the desired deadlines;
- I saved time on individual stories about the book to my surroundings;
- I immediately received the expected, and even more powerful than I hoped, stimulus to continue in the form of sincere inspiring feedback, comments, and even book orders.

Structural features.

The structure (also the Contents) of the book.

I don't think any author ever writes a list of chapters that remain immovable monoliths, carved from stone from start to finish. So, the Structure of my book had changed and had been reviewed several times until it became as you see it now — the result of creative search and 'operational-tactical developments'.

Epigraphs.

I love winged phrases from famous people. They summarize the experience and intellectual achievements of humanity's best, whom we should and need to emulate. So, for me, it's like in the military on the parade ground, when a senior officer comes out, and the sergeant commands: 'Alignment! ON! The middle!'. In this way, I give the reader a signal in literary form: align with this wisdom, then I will add a bit of my modest content.

Introductory and concluding parts of chapters.

You may have noticed that each Chapter in the book begins and ends with italicized text. I think, having read the book, you also understood the content of that text. It was an idea of my mentor Roman Kuziuk to present excerpts from my real life at the beginning and end of the topic to support various theses in the Chapter.

In this way, it helped make the book more 'alive' and in some places to reinforce the theoretical expositions of the Chapters with practical cases, situations, events, acts, and reflections on the given topic.

Conclusions and principles.

Always and in everything, both as for a civilian manager and a commander of various scales, it is critically important to highlight what is important, relevant, and main. So, this book could not do without presenting summaries. Without them, I believe, such work would be incomplete.

INSIGHTS that arose in the course of writing.

Accurate 'author's' phrases.

Once during another brainstorm, Roman noted: 'This phrase of yours came out very 'tasty'. Let's highlight it.' And so, during the writing of the book, we accumulated several phrases that in their content and form carry a certain 'charge' and it was me who managed to formulate them. Roman calls such things 'thoughtful achievements', a broader and more known term — insight. It's possible that a particular reader will 'highlight' something else, closer to his experience and worldview. Well, as an Author (Roman insists that this word should be used with a capital letter :) I see it this way!

Also, interesting expressions of contributors we tried to highlight.

Stable expressions through the "filter of war."

Also, a kind of insight for me was the understanding that certain winged phrases, expressions, clichés began to sound and be perceived differently in the conditions of war. This also became unexpected, interesting content, which I wanted to highlight for the reader and over which it might be useful to ponder.

Tools.

Similar to the well-known expression, "all is fair in love and war," I use literally every available tool. For motivation communication with coach Roman, public promises in posts on LinkedIn and Facebook, and conversations with experts both in Ukraine and abroad. For working directly on the text — phone, voice recorder, tablet, PC, even paper and pen, online and offline software. For inspiration...I don't even know where it comes from in a mode of constant shortage of time, sleep, strength, and rest. Probably, from all these circumstances, which try to metaphorically "squeeze" me, I willfully "squeeze out" content. Also, His Majesty Deadline. A great managerial tool, friends, great...

Additionally, before sitting down to write the book, I read several books about writing, notably "On Writing: A Memoir of the Craft" by Stephen King and "On Writing Well" by William Zinsser. Mykhailo Fedorov recommended King's book, which, while not directly influencing my writing style, certainly sets the right mood.

By the way, these Zinsser quotes can set the mood for you, too:

- Show your 'I', and the goal of your story will speak for itself. Believe in your uniqueness and views. Writing is kind of an act of egoism. Realize it and move on. Every successful book should prompt the readers to one interesting thought they didn't have before. Not two thoughts, not five, but one.
- How can we all free ourselves from linguistic chaos? We need to rid our consciousness of it. Clean thoughts — clean writing. One is impossible without the other. You won't write well if everything is confused in your head.

- People will write better and more willingly if they talk about what they love.
- Don't try to change your voice to match the topic. Develop a single voice that readers will recognize, a voice they will enjoy not only for its mellifluousness but also for the absence of "sounds" that spoil the tone: carelessness, arrogance, and clichés.
- Your writing is inextricably linked to your character. If you have "strong" spiritual values, your texts will also be strong.

Writing a book is like talking to yourself, pulling out of memory and thoughts what's important, looking at it and fixing it. It involves making conclusions and translating the most important reflections into more convenient shelves for daily use. This process is very useful for understanding yourself as a person and for further personal development.

Filling.

It's difficult to envision modern literature without the element of visualization. I firmly believe that certain ideas in the book require "decoding" or "enhancement" through illustrations, photos, and infographics. In the printed edition, incorporating QR codes is essential. These codes provide a convenient way for smartphone users to access additional links related to the book's content.

My ambition for this book extends beyond Ukraine's borders. I yearn to share our struggles and victories with the world — to relay our story to individuals in Warsaw, Oslo, Berlin, London, Ohio, Toronto, Hong Kong, and Singapore. It is a tale of leadership and management practices forged in the crucible of conflict, which deserves to be heard by a global audience.

When creating digital solutions, we focus on the mobile first approach

To realize this vision, I collaborated with Matt MacFarlane, employing his innovative translation methodology. We utilized the sophisticated Langchain language processing framework, augmented by Meta SeamlessM4T and GPT4 transformers, ensuring my work's essence and depth were faithfully preserved for an English-speaking audience.

This comprehensive translation approach combined machine learning, artificial intelligence, and the insights of native English speakers. The outcome was a translation that not only maintained accuracy but also resonated with the cultural subtleties of the original text.

Roman Kuziuk

Founder and CEO of the Business Literature Publishing House "The Ultimate Beneficiary"

Tetiana Yashkina

Philanthropist and Founder of the weapons store chain "Okhota"

Haakon Rian Mansent Ueland

Social Worker, Musician, and Author

Håkan Jyde

Director of Scania Ukraine

Charles Mok

Visiting Scholar at the Global Digital Policy Incubator of the Cyber Policy Center at Stanford University

Jan Dirk Geertsema

Author, Consultant, and Lecturer of the course "Leadership and Human Logic" at the University of California and Kyiv-Mohyla Business School

PROFESSIONS REPRESENTED BY THE CONTRIBUTORS:

Auditing, forensics 1   Nuclear engineering 1

Journalism 1   Medicine 1   Education and science 2

Sales management 1   Management 3   Coaching 1

Public administration 2   Consulting 4   Technology 1

Business owner 1   IT sales 1   Data Science 1

Banking 1   Information technology 1

Content marketing 4   International business 1

Entrepreneurship 1

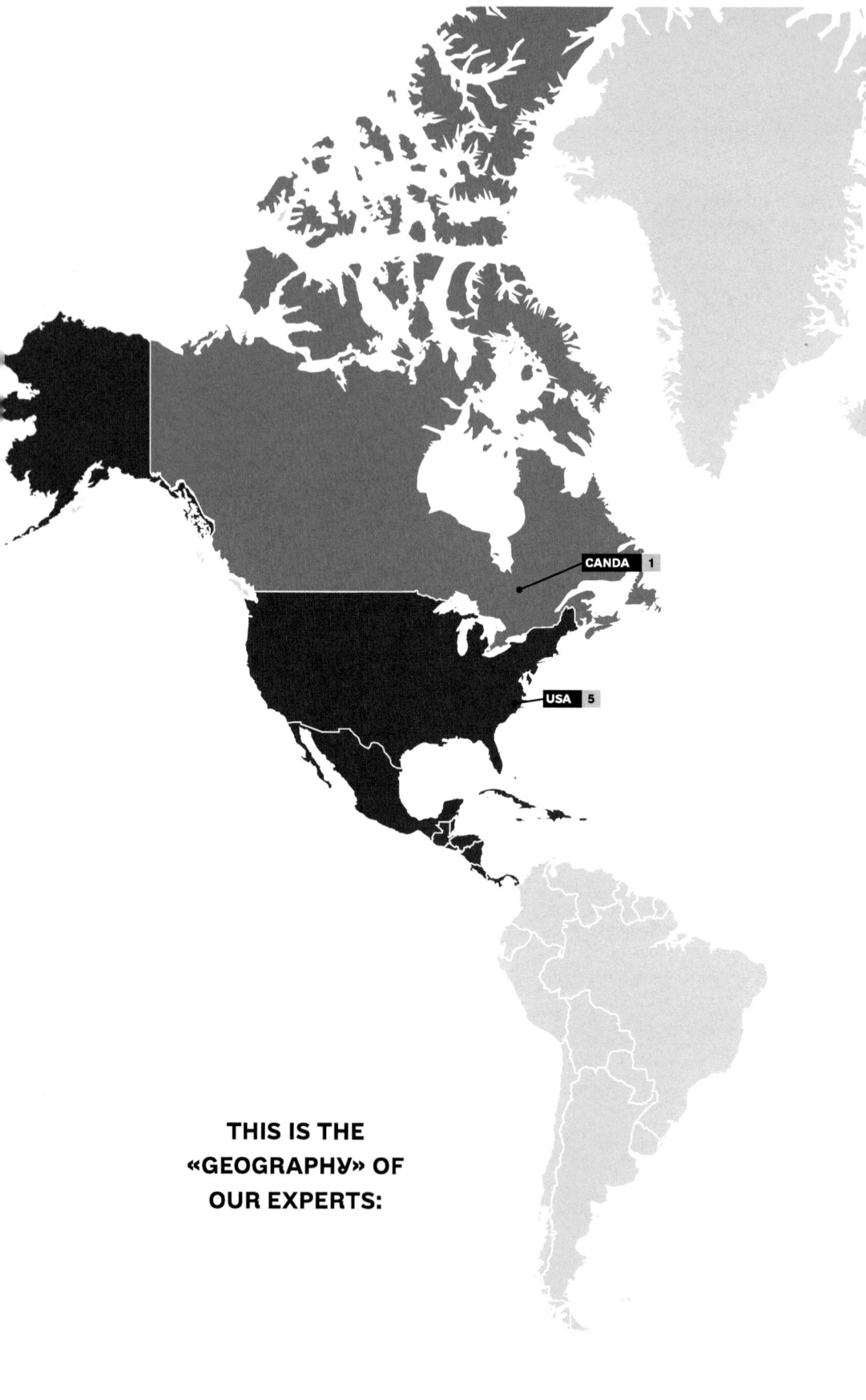

CANDA 1

USA 5

THIS IS THE
«GEOGRAPHY» OF
OUR EXPERTS:

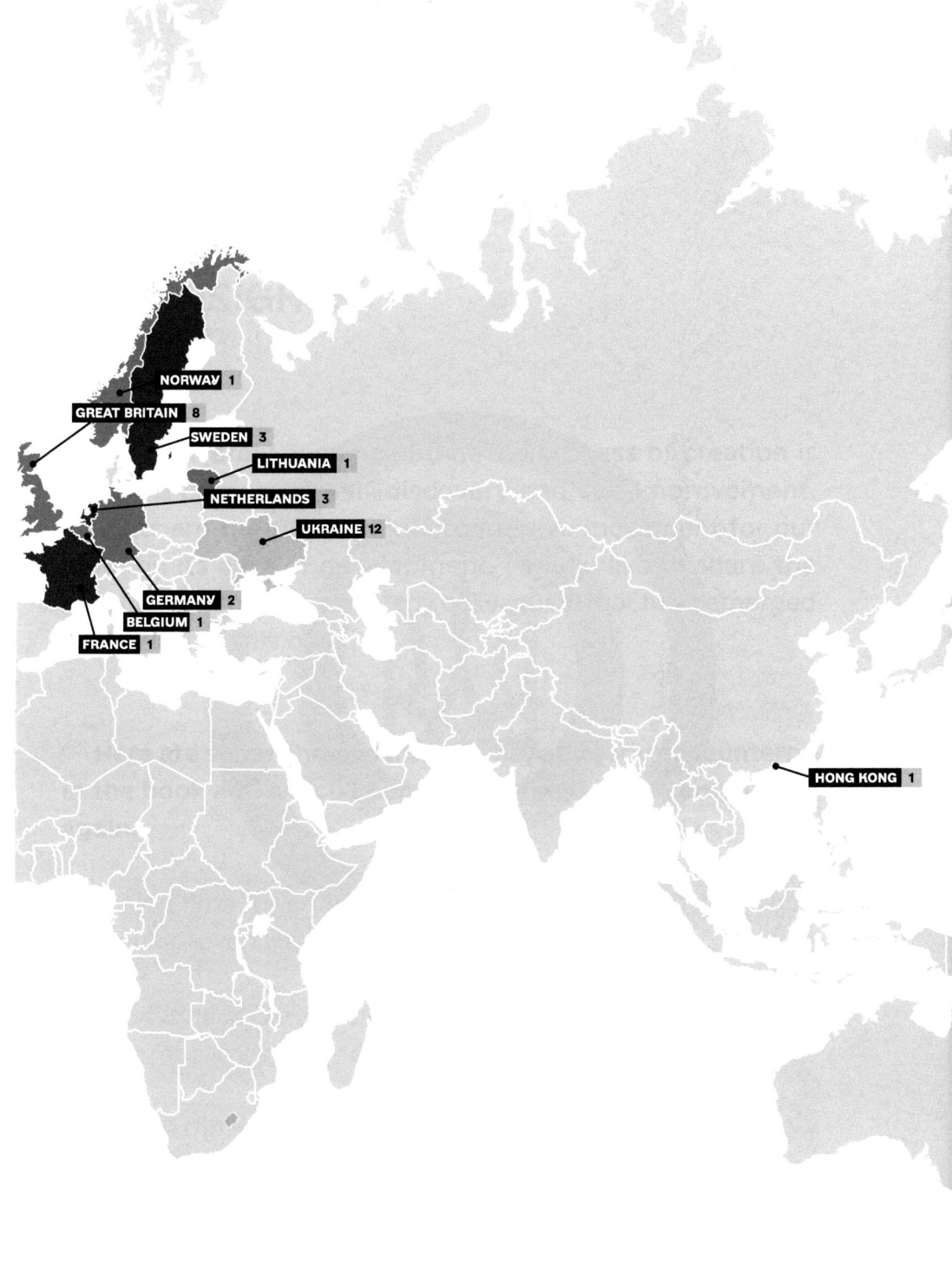

NORWAY 1

GREAT BRITAIN 8

SWEDEN 3

LITHUANIA 1

NETHERLANDS 3

UKRAINE 12

GERMANY 2

BELGIUM 1

FRANCE 1

HONG KONG 1

Helicopter view — *Valued for its ability to look at problems from different perspectives. Today, it immediately brings to mind military helicopters.*

Sharpen the saw — *A phrase by Stephen Covey about continual education and improvement. During war, it's more about sharpening the sword or strengthening the shield: "sharpen the sword (temper the steel)."*

ABOUT THE AUTHOR
ПРО АВТОРА

If you are a leader, if you want to be one, you have to read. You cannot grow in your leadership without learning from others and that requires reading.

Margaret Fuller

Kostiantyn began his managerial career in the banking sector of the 2000s, a time of active growth, focusing initially on customer service, sales management, and business development, first in offline and then online environments. For most of his 15-year career in retail business, he concentrated on creating innovative products and services for customers. This involved competing with top market players, fulfilling the ambitious business goals of shareholders, pursuing self-development, and exploring the world for both himself and his family. This work was interesting, providing the necessary inspiration, motivation, and support for professional growth and a comfortable life.

However, Kostiantyn's motivation began to shift with his personal development and changing circumstances — crises, the arrival of children, the annexation of Ukrainian Crimea by Russia, and ultimately, the war. His priorities also shifted towards more global goals. He realized that the development of Ukraine and socially beneficial initiatives were much more important than any individual achievements.

For a long time, he didn't see the opportunity to change the country from within the inefficient, cumbersome, and corrupt state apparatus, and was hesitant to enter public service. However, he started investing time and resources into developing the environment and people around him. This changed at the beginning of President Zelensky's tenure, when Kostiantyn felt that there was an opportunity for real reform of the Ukrainian state. With a critical mass of people in power sharing relevant values, he decided to contribute to the ambitious and noble goal of developing the country.

Kostiantyn joined the State Property Fund of Ukraine as a deputy responsible for the efficient operation of the regional network. These were not the kind of branches he was used to seeing in competitive banks — no advertising on facades, convenient premises, or quality service. Instead, they were diverse spaces located in various old buildings, where getting a consultation from employees, especially leaders, was incredibly difficult.

In two years, his small team managed to strengthen management, increase the efficiency of these regional representations, and contribute to their client-oriented development, transparency, and digitalization. They also built open interactions with the business environment, communities, regional state administrations, journalists, and media. Without marketing expenses, the regional branches conducted 806 events in two years, reaching over 17,000 people in the regions. There was probably no significant regional or national business association with which they did not meet to explain how easy it is to participate in privatization through Prozorro.Sales[15] auctions, where maximum information disclosure is ensured[16].

339 broadcasts on regional TV and radio channels were initiated, further increasing coverage. The formats varied from briefings and interviews to press breakfasts. This allowed for a significant increase in investment compared to previous

---

15 prozorro.sale    16 privatization.gov.ua

years, fulfilling plans for small privatization and leasing, and achieving the biggest successes in 20 years in resolving the issue of non-statutory property — housing, infrastructure, and civil protection facilities that had been ownerless since the privatization of the 90s.

When Kostiantyn was concluding his work at the State Property Fund of Ukraine, only in 2021, through 1,553 small privatization auctions, the expected income was 4.4 billion UAH against a plan of 3.7 billion UAH. 2,129 participants took part in such auctions, whereas in 2018 there were only 715, some of which were fictitious.

Joining the Ministry of Social Policy in January 2022, he focused on the digital transformation of the social sphere — the development of the Unified Information System, intended to centrally administer all types of state social support. This system replaced the old systems created in the 90s and allowed for information exchanges with other state registries and systems. In simple terms, thanks to these exchanges, megabytes of data began to circulate between organizations instead of relying on citizens physically presenting documents to each agency, thereby making services fast and automatic. This system also allowed The Ministry of Social Policy to start moving social services to the Diia portal and app, enabling citizens to use them remotely.

The full-scale invasion adjusted plans, but the team managed to act asymmetrically and sometimes proactively, meeting the challenges of war. You'll find a general overview of this in the book, but not too detailed to avoid making the book seem like specialized literature for experts in social services and digitalization.

A text about the author would not be complete without a paragraph about Kostiantyn's education, complementing information about his professional background. After completing secondary education, he began his professional education at Zaporizhzhia Electrical Technical College, where he chose the specialty "Installation and Operation of Electrical Equipment" based on his father's advice. Following this, he pursued parallel secondary technical education in "Enterprise Economics," and enrolledt in higher education for "Computer Networks and Systems" with parallel studies in "Management."

Kostiantyn continued to learn throughout his life, obtaining an MBA from the Kiev-Mohyla Business School (kmbs), participating in a course at the Ukrainian Corporate Governance Academy, attending Aspen seminars, and completing various short-term courses, including training as a UAV operator in 2023. Also, he serves as an honorary professor at Alfred Nobel University's International Business School.

In conclusion, it's important to highlight that in addition to his diverse experiences, Kostiantyn often draws parallels between his association with marathon running and enduring the challenges of the war. He has participated in 11 marathons and 28 half-marathons, demonstrating perseverance by never dropping out of a race, despite not being the fastest runner.

Thanks to Deputy Prime Minister Mykhailo Fedorov and the Ministry of Digital Transformation of Ukraine, numerous individuals in the government and civil society rallied around the vision of creating the most convenient country in the world in terms of state services, making all services just a click away. Together with digitalizers from various ministries and departments, we are doing this even during the invasion; as it's not only about the efficiency of the state and the comfort of people but also about safety.

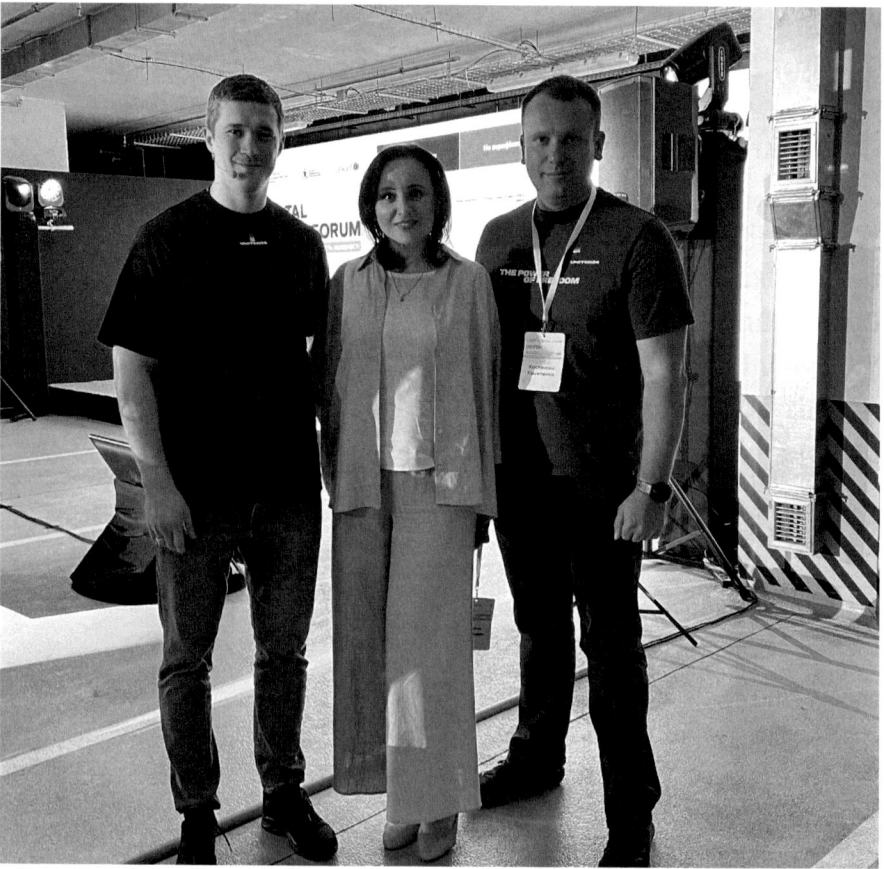

Mykhailo Fedorov, Oksana Zholnovych
and Kostiantyn Koshelenko

Breakthrough digital solutions emerge when there is a demand for them, and in this regard, I was fortunate to work with the team at the Ministry of Social Policy. The digital first approach inside drives and is supported by Minister Oksana Zholnovych, and the entire team of deputies — Daryna Marchak, Nazar Tanasyshyn, Ulyana Tokareva, and Iryna Postolovska — all start their innovations in social support with ideas about digital solutions, as do all other members of our team.

Top managers of the Ministry of Social Policy

Of course, I could have done nothing without the digital team of the Ministry and colleagues — Oleksandr Kalinin, Valerii Shtaba, Liliia Lishnianska, Pavlo Bortnikov, Tetiana Khomosh, Iryna Lutsenko, Oleksii Melnikov, Nataliia Morhun, Denys Panchenko, Khrystyna Vitko, Andrii Matviichuk, Oksana Ovramenko, Oksana Satanovska, Yurii Lobunets, Viktor Klymenko, Liudmyla Khlan, Nataliia Bogachova, Bohdan

Skuratovskyi, Serhii Beliakov, Nataliia Kurash, Yuliia Krasovska, Alina Andronova, Mariia Sakuta, Valeriia Yeshchenko, Alina Kyrylychenko and many others who did not stop in development and were not afraid of overload and difficult tasks.

Thanks to Dariia Herasymchuk for initiating the complex of adoption services on the Diia portal and supporting its creation from the first month of the full-scale invasion, which allowed consulting potential adopters already in the third month of the great war.

We could not have done so much with limited resources if not for the partners with whom we created digital solutions for social assistance and services during this period.

In various areas, we were helped with resources and expertise by UN World Food Programme, UNICEF, Committee for Open Democracy: (Help Ukraine project), East Europe Foundation (TAPAS and EGAP programs), PrivatBank Foundation "Helping is Easy", Cullen International and other organizations. But behind each organization are people, so I sincerely thank David Thomas, Matthew Hollingworth, Oleksandr Beiko, Marat Sahin, Paul von Kittlitz, Olena Kopyl, Kateryna Martynenko, Viktor Liakh, Yuliia Zaplavna, Danylo Molchanov, Jean Cullen, Sebastian Kulczyk and their teams, partners, and sponsors.

The eSupport platform, now encompassing over 5,400 charity volunteers from 54 countries, owes its reach to those who assisted in its early development and became its ambassadors. Derek Elder, Andrea McKinney, Serhii Vovk, Irina Nikonchuk, Pavlo Kyrychenko, Hanna Bobino, Pavlo Rudyka, Dmitro Braginets, Michael Keyes, Mark Ruffalo, Andreas Keßler, Ulrich Sattler, Marcin Figlus, Vasyl Virastyuk, and Alona Bulba, thank you.

eSupport team

Special thanks to those who supported my initiatives to help civilians and the military. I will not write their names because acknowledgement of such assistance would place the lives of these international friends at risk. Due to the selfless actions of these people, by the time of writing the book, 2 pickups, 2 minibuses, a sniper rifle, 31 drones, and some accessories were provided to the Armed Forces of Ukraine, and hundreds of Ukrainians received help.

By the way, some of the people mentioned contributed in various capacities, while others assisted in every possible way. In the meantime, I will continue to express my appreciation here: Alfonso Fernandez Muniz, Nicolas Rodriguez, João Miguel Ferreira, Jacques Quigley, Artem Skorupych, Oleksii Tsal-Tsalko, Brigitte Issel, Lionel Felix, Charles Tine, Dmitry Lampert, Martin Vesper, Piotr Zayka, Howard Boyle, Oksana Sen, Raymond Werner, Mia Kolmodin, Maridjin Marcus,

Paul Woren, Jeff Haber, Petr Chlechovitz, Boris Mizhen, Sally Schmidt, Arvydas Siaudvytis, Miriam Semrau, Jacobs Minten, Paul Rozvadovsky, Dirk Heberich, Mariia Chornobai, Hort Schauerte, Nicolas Andreyis, Stefani Brand, Leo Shin, Stefvan Dorigh, Darius Tsal-Tsalko, Andrii Stetsenko, Serhii Stetsenko, Joanie Gosliccy, Olena Fadeeva, Carol Collins, Sarah Allen, Peter Schmidt-Hansen, Dr. Iris Weigel, Elvira Kaegi, Victoria Wilette, Oleksii Avramenko, Anton Avramenko, Stamatios Kristopolus, Rob Dakster, Arnaud Contival, Sameem Monzaviyan, Tetiana Avramenko, Ingus Ostrovskis, and Leander van Gorsel.

The transfer of a pick-up truck for the military, which was brought on the way from a business trip to Brussels

And, of course, I extend the greatest gratitude to the men and women who have defended and continue to defend Ukraine with arms on the front lines. Without these heroes, there would be no rear in which it would be possible to work and perform the tasks I wrote about in this book.

Kurt Matsler

Open Strategy: Mastering
Disruption from Outside
the C-Suite

Tristan Evans

Post-War Foreign Direct
Investment Into Ukraine

Myroslav Kobylianskyi

My Mariupol and the world
around

ACKNOWLEDGEMENTS

Andrii Onistrat

How I Lo$t the Bank

Roman Kuziuk

Business Detective
"Ultimate Beneficiary"

THE LIBRARY OF A MANAGER IN TIMES OF WAR

Бібліотека менеджера у часи війни

My work would be incomplete if, during the writing of this book, I didn't make an effort to document as much literature as possible that I sincerely recommend for you to explore. So, here are my lists for your attention:

Bibliography:

- The Most In-Demand Skills for 2023. Jen Dewar.[16]
- How CEOs Manage Time by Michael E. Porter and Nitin Nohria, Harvard Business Review (July–August 2018)
- From Good to Great by Jim Collins
- Agile for Yourself by Jay D. Meier
- Managing Stress by David Lewis
- Scrum: Learn to Do Twice as Much in Half the Time by Jeff Sutherland
- The 7 Habits of Highly Effective People by Stephen Covey

---

16   Jen Dewar "The Most In-Demand Skills for 2023"

- Principles by Ray Dalio
- Marketing Wars by Jack Trout and Al Ries
- The Power of Now: A Guide to Spiritual Enlightenment by Eckhart Tolle
- Manifesto for Agile Software Development.[17]
- Armored Mind: Combat Stress and the Psychology of Extreme Situations by Kostiantyn Ulianov
- Colorful Management: Evolution of Thinking, Leadership, and Management by Valerii Pekar
- The Sports Businessman by Roman Kuziuk
- Reforms During War: How Ukraine Digitizes the Social Sphere.[18]
- David's Victory: Discipline of Disproportionate Victory by Adrian Slywotzky
- The Project 50 (Reinventing Work): Fifty Ways to Transform Every 'Task' into a Project That Matters! by Tom Peters
- The Goal: A Process of Ongoing Improvement by Eliyahu M. Goldratt and Jeff Cox
- Homo Ludens: A Study of the Play-Element in Culture by Johan Huizinga
- On Writing Well: The Classic Guide to Writing Nonfiction by William Zinsser
- On Writing: A Memoir of the Craft by Stephen King

---

17 Manifesto for Agile Software Development

18 Реформи під час війни.

List of Recommended Literature from the Author:

- Discipline Equals Freedom by Jocko Willink
- Battlegrounds: The Fight to Defend the Free World by H.R. McMaster
- Team of Teams: New Rules of Engagement for a Complex World by Stanley McChrystal, Tantum Collins, David Silverman, Chris Fussell
- Leading from Purpose by Nick Craig
- Leading Manchester United: How to Become a Champion Manager by Alex Ferguson
- My Boss is an Idiot by Thomas Erikson
- Never Stop by Mari Karachina
- Thinking in Systems: A Primer by Donella Meadows
- On Writing: A Memoir of the Craft by Stephen King
- Be Useful by Arnold Schwarzenegger
- The Restless Wave: Good Times, Just Causes, Great Fights, and Other Appreciations by John McCain and Mark Salter
- The American Imperative: Reclaiming Global Leadership through Soft Power by Daniel F. Runde
- How to Run a Government: So that Citizens Benefit and Taxpayers Don't Go Crazy by Michael Barber
- Atlas Shrugged by Ayn Rand
- Animal Farm by George Orwell
- The Emotional Swings of War by Volodymyr Stanchyshyn
- Battle for Kyiv by Serhii Rudenko
- The Return of History: The Russian-Ukrainian War by Serhii Plokhy
- Invasion: Behind the Bloody War of Russia and Ukraine's Struggle for Survival by Luke Harding

List of Recommended Literature from Expert Contributors:

- Principles, Auditor Chronicles, 2nd book by Rey Dalio
- Man's Search for Meaning by Viktor Frankl
- My Life and Work by Henry Ford
- Marketing Management by Philip Kotler
- Cascades: How to Create a Movement that Drives Transformational Change by Greg Satell
- Life Under Fire by Jason Fox & 12 Rules of Life by Jordan B Peterson
- The 8th Habit: From Effectiveness to Greatness by Stephen R. Covey
- Long Game by Rush Doshi
- Faster Together by Laura Stack
- The Conversations with God-books
- How To Win Friends and Influence People by Dale Carnegie
- The Black Swan by Nassim Taleb
- Homo Deus: A Brief History of Tomorrow by Yuval Noah Harari
- Collapse: How Societies Choose to Fail or Succeed by Jared Diamond
- Essentialism: The Disciplined Pursuit of Less by Greg McKeown
- So Many to Choose From – But I'll Go with 'Getting to Yes' by Fisher & Ury
- Good to Great by Jim Collins
- Psychology of War by George T. W. Patrick, David S. Jordan

- QUANTUM SUCCESS: 7 Essential Laws for a Thriving, Joyful, and Prosperous Relationship with Work and Money by Christy Whitman
- Why Nations Fail? The Origins of Power, Wealth, and Poverty by Daron Acemoglu and James Robinson

AFTERWORD — ATTENTION IS ALL UKRAINE NEEDS

By Matt MacFarlane

How We Translated "Management in Times of War" Using Attention and AI, and How Attention and the Power of Transformers Will Help Ukraine Harness Industry 4.0 to Win the War

You and I are born screaming and crying into a scary and unstructured world. Crying, because we have no words. Screaming, because we do not understand. But soon, we come into contact with structure. Structure adds context; structure adds meaning. Family is the first structure we encounter. Language is another. Some structures unite us. Others divide us. Echoing the metaphor of the Tower of Babel, language has historically served to divide us. Certain languages, such as English, are associated with better outcomes, while other — not so much. In some countries, certain subjects are taught in languages other than the native language of the people. In Ukraine, before the war, courses in math, science, and technology may have been taught in English or Russian. Most of the textbooks for these subjects were in English or Russian. And we have accepted this as par for the course. We have accepted the structures imposed upon us and have been powerless to meaningfully push back, assert our independence, as well as assert our own structures and our vision of the world.

And we were drowning. Drowning in the volume, variety, and velocity of data flung at us from every direction. But no more. In 2017, Google published its seminal research paper, Attention is All You Need, and introduced the world to the Transformer: a new class of machine learning model. Transformers change everything. They are industrialized models with billion and trillion parameters. ChatGPT is one. Google Gemini is another. These are just the tip of the spear: what works for text and natural language also works for images, sequences of images, videos, and more. Multimodal models like these bridge the gaps between language, art, and vision, heralding a new era of interconnectedness.

The Fourth Industrial Revolution is all about connecting things to things: computers to computers, computers to humans, and humans to humans.

In the Digital Revolution, which we have so recently left behind, our unity gave us strength. Our homogeneity —everyone on the same internet, everyone on the same hardware, marching together to the beat of the drum —was the source of our power.

But Industry 4.0 is completely different. Industry 4.0 is paradoxical if you do not understand the distributed systems around us that keep us prosperous and free.

Our strength no longer lies in our homogeneity. Instead, it stems from the degrees of our differences, complex interconnections, and disparate passions. These elements, when united, foster a union that keeps us free.

This technological leap is central to the Fourth Industrial Revolution and represents a shift from centralized structures of power and information to distributed, networked systems that empower individuals and communities. AI models like Transformers are dismantling language barriers, fostering deeper understanding and collaboration between nations, and offering tools for nations like Ukraine to assert their independence and cultural identity against foreign narratives and propaganda.

Russia's authoritarian regime has long attempted to exert control over Ukraine through cultural and linguistic oppression. The "The Russian Way" is a systematic attempt to dismantle Ukrainian identity, language, and culture.

In the realm of foreign policy, these technological advancements are reshaping diplomatic strategies by improving communication and access to information globally. Ukraine's ability to share its perspective internationally without language barriers challenges Russia's narrative dominance. The use of AI in documenting and distributing real-time data from conflict zones counters misinformation campaigns. This is altering how the international community responds to Russian military actions in Ukraine.

With son Stanislav passed
a drone operator course

The finish line of the Lviv Half Marathon.
Autumn 2022.

A meeting in Kyiv with Boas Kragtwijk, who ran the distance from Amsterdam to Kyiv, collecting funds for an ambulances for Ukraine.

At the presentation of the Diya.Engine platform of state registers with Yuriy Konovalov and Bohdan Skurativskyi

The digital team of the Ministry of Social Policy on Unity Day,
February 16, 2022. A week before the full-scale war.

With the Dutch volunteer Leander van Gorsel in the background,
the car in which he himself brought humanitarian aid

With Enoh T. Ebong Director of www.ustda.gov
on a mission to Washington D.C.

Volunteer Ingus Ostrovskis, who regularly brings technical assistance to Ukraine and the
Head of the National Social Service Vasyl Lutsik, Ambassador of Latvia to Ukraine Ilgvars
Kļava, Kostyantyn Koshelenko and director of www.ioc.gov.ua Yuriy Konovalov

We hold a meeting with the Unicef team during the air alert: Kostyantyn Koshelenko, Hanna Prorok, Iryna Postolovska, Daryna Marchak, Murat Sahin, Paul von Kittlitz, Jean Choi

With the team of the charity fund "Ukrainian code" — ambassadors of the eDopomoga platform — Vasyl Virastyuk, Anton Shkarupa, Pavlo Bortnikov, Kostyantyn Koshelenko, Alona Bulba, Andriy Perehrest